THE TWO LOLITAS

◆

MICHAEL MAAR

VERSO

London · New York

This paperback edition first published by Verso 2017
First published by Verso 2005
© Michael Maar 2005, 2017
Introduction © Daniel Kehlmann 2017
Translation © Perry Anderson 2005, 2017
Appendix I translation © Will Hobson 2005, 2017
Appendix II was first published in the German magazine *Cicero*, and later published in English
by the *Paris Review*. We reproduce it here with thanks to that publication for permission.
Appendix II translation © Daniel Kehlmann 2017
Photographs of Nabokov on pages 15 and 47 © Vladimir Nabokov Estate
Photograph of Nabokov on page 51 © Jochen Richter/Bayerisches Fernsehen

The moral rights of the authors and translators have been asserted

1 3 5 7 9 10 8 6 4 2

Verso
UK: 6 Meard Street, London W1F 0EG
US: 20 Jay Street, Suite 1010, Brooklyn, 11201
versobooks.com

Verso is the imprint of New Left Books

ISBN-13: 978-1-78663-184-8
ISBN-13: 978-1-78663-185-5 (UK EBK)
ISBN-13: 978-1-78663-186-2 (US EBK)

British Library Cataloguing in Publication Data
A catalogue record for this book is available from the British Library

Library of Congress Cataloging-in-Publication Data

Names: Maar, Michael, author. | Kehlmann, Daniel, 1975– translator, writer of
    preface, interviewer. | Anderson, Perry, translator. | Hobson, Will,
    translator of appendix. | Lichberg, Heinz von. Lolita. English. |
    Lichberg, Heinz von. Atomite. English.
Title: The two Lolitas / Michael Maar.
Other titles: Lolita und der deutsche Leutnant. English
Description: Brooklyn : Verso, 2017. | 'Translation: Perry Anderson;
    translation of Appendix: Will Hobson' –Verso title page. | A reissue of
    the 2005 Verso edition, with a new preface and an interview with Nabokov
    by Daniel Kehlmann. | Includes bibliographical references. | Originally
    published in German as Lolita und der deutsche Leutnant.
Identifiers: LCCN 2017015964 | ISBN 9781786631848 (paperback)
Subjects: LCSH: Nabokov, Vladimir Vladimirovich, 1899–1977. Lolita. |
    Lichberg, Heinz von. Lolita. | BISAC: LITERARY CRITICISM / Semiotics &
    Theory. | LITERARY CRITICISM / Books & Reading.
Classification: LCC PS3527.A15 L633 2017 | DDC 813/.54—dc23
LC record available at https://lccn.loc.gov/2017015964

Typeset in Perpetua by YHT Ltd, London
Printed and bound by CPI Group (UK) Ltd, Croydon, CR0 4YY

CONTENTS

**INTRODUCTION BY
DANIEL KEHLMANN**

I confess that Michael Maar's discovery about *Lolita* has become an obsession of mine. I've no solution to offer, and to be quite frank, I don't even have a convincing theory; but at the same time I can't accept that the riddle is unsolvable. Of course, for people uninterested in the labyrinthine art and adventurous life of Vladimir Nabokov, this doesn't matter – but for a Nabokov-lover, Maar's discovery is so astonishing that you would need to have firmly opted for ignorance to maintain it was unimportant.

I won't describe Maar's impressive detective work here; you can read it for yourself in his own elegant prose. I'd just like to mention two things that are always brought up in connection with it. First of all, the whole business could of course be pure accident. In theory this wouldn't be impossible. It could be accidental that two central characters in works by two writers unknown to one another are called Lolita; it could be pure chance that each is a landlady's daughter, and it could likewise be by chance that both authors wrote stories in which an inventor presents a minister of war with a weapon of mass destruction, and introduced two closely related men called Waltz, a name which is not exactly common. In pure logic, there is nothing against this. But it is certainly improbable – so improbable that almost any other hypothesis is more likely. Besides, Maar discovered after the first publication of this book (there is a footnote on this in the new edition) that Lichberg was related to Nabokov's Berlin landlady – a woman whose family is still mentioned in Nabokov's letters to his wife Véra years after he moved from the house. And so, to put it very cautiously, it is at least not absurd to assume there is a causal connection.

Secondly, wherever this causal connection may lie, it has nothing to do with plagiarism. This should go without saying, but still needs to be stated loud and clear. When Maar published his discovery for the first time, newspapers across the world reported 'accusations of cribbing' against Vladimir Nabokov. As was only to be expected, a few Nabokov experts felt themselves moved by a kind of reflex to defend the great man against an accusation that no one had actually made – most of them simply saying that Lolita was after all a common name, and failing to mention the many other coincidences: 'Nabokov family rejects plagiarism claim' was a headline in the *Guardian* in April 2004. When in April 2016, in an interview for the online edition of the *Paris Review*, I asked Michael Maar, 'Is this about plagiarism?' he answered, 'Of course not.' And yet more than one literary magazine referred to this discussion, reprinted here as Appendix II, with the outcry that a German literary critic was raising accusations of plagiarism against Nabokov. It seems as if the concept 'plagiarism' is so strong that it overrides any logical operator, any qualification, even a clear denial.

Superfluous as this is, it must therefore be restated: What Maar discovered not only has nothing to do with plagiarism, but is its very opposite. If I name a character in a novel 'Leopold Bloom', I am not plagiarizing James Joyce's *Ulysses*: I am deliberately referencing it. Had Nabokov simply been inspired by the (bad) novelist Lichberg, it would have been easy for him to cover his tracks. But given an essential aspect of the concordance lies precisely in the characters' names, we have by definition not theft but rather deliberate indication.

But for whom is this indication designed? And why? Neither in personal nor artistic terms do we find anything about Lichberg that might have influenced or even interested the uncompromising master Nabokov. What is it we are overlooking, then? What is there that we don't know? A reference is an act of communication, but with whom was Nabokov communicating here, given that Lichberg had long been dead when *Lolita* was published, and his book had been out of print for years? Communication with spirits may well be an important theme in Nabokov, but here we would be in the realm of pure speculation.

And if we simply shrug our shoulders and say: 'I don't care!'? The urge to do so would certainly be understandable. If a similar question had arisen with Hemingway or Hamsun, it would indeed have been a matter of indifference; but Nabokov is precisely the key author of the cipher, the grand master of reference, the very one out of all novelists of classic modernity who signals most tirelessly to the reader that in his work every detail is important and needs deciphering.

And so we are supposed to solve the mystery; Nabokov himself schooled us to do so with his understanding of literary works as highly complex puzzles. What then are we to do? We can at least, while awaiting new discoveries and new detectives, read Michael Maar's book and bear the confusion it arouses in us with stoical curiosity.

THE TWO LOLITAS

A fter the phone call came through, the publisher climbed on to the table. An anonymous friend inside the Home Office had rung with the news: the government had decided against prosecution. No one responsible for the novel to be published the next day would go to jail. The three hundred guests invited to the Ritz were jubilant.

For a month, a copy of the scandalous work had been under examination by the Director of Public Prosecutions; twenty thousand copies were waiting in bookshops, to be either sold out or quietly pulped. The charge hanging over the publisher was dissemination of an immoral work. In the House of Commons, the Attorney-General had warned Nigel Nicolson that publication of it could land him behind bars. The author's wife joked that her husband would spend Christmas either in Italy or at the Old Bailey.

The party held in London on 5 November 1959 was a climactic moment in the career of a novel that would turn the life of its author upside-down. Five American houses had rejected the manuscript, and urgently advised him against publication. The French publisher who eventually accepted the book specialized in erotica, trading in titles like *Tender Thighs* and *Memoirs of a Woman of Pleasure*. Graham Greene, writing in the *Times Literary Supplement* in 1955, was the first to notify the world that the two green volumes released by Olympia Press were great literature. On that November evening four years later, even the British government certified that the book in question was not pornography, but art. Thereafter the triumphal march of the novel was not to be halted. The cheers that went up when Nigel Nicolson clambered on to the table and announced the news could be heard blocks away.[1]

This part of the story is well-known. The following, unknown part has elements of the fantastic about it – indeed, may sound like a tall tale. Yet no overinventive author but rather life itself is responsible for its volutes and arabesques. It is a true story, and we will begin with its end.

Eight years before the big party in London, the local paper in Lübeck announced that one of its contributors had passed away:

Last Wednesday, after a short illness, our colleague and collaborator Heinz von Eschwege-Lichberg died. The pen

---

[1] Stacy Schiff, *Véra (Mrs Vladimir Nabokov)*, New York, Random House 1999, pp. 257–8.

has finally fallen from the hands of one of the best-known personalities in German journalism.[2]

The condolences of the editorialist were only slightly overstated at the time. Today the fame of the deceased has faded, to put it

---

[2] There follows this more detailed obituary: 'Heinz von Eschwege-Lichberg was an equestrian. Horses were his great passion. He loved and had to ride. When as a cavalry officer he had to take off his uniform after the First World War, it was all but logical that he should have swung himself into the saddle of Pegasus to continue his charges. He went to Berlin, to Scherl-Verlag, where the *Berliner Lokal-Anzeiger* offered him an ample arena in which to take his winged steed through every kind of exercise. Berlin and Berliners, with their brightness, warmth and cheek, became his journalistic loves; he depicted them with humour and sarcasm, but always with words from the heart and to the heart. He never denied the cavalier of the old school, who indeed exposed the many small weaknesses of his fellow human beings with the wisdom of a philosopher and made merry over them, but always had a forgiving smile to spare for them. He wanted to make people both gay and reflective. He took life extremely seriously – but not more seriously than was absolutely necessary. So he wandered as a humorous talker of 'small things' through the world of Berlin journalism, until the general call-up of 1936, when his vocation as a soldier beckoned him again. It was only after the collapse of the country that he mounted Pegasus again, this time in Lübeck, the town he thought closest to his Berlin. The reader of the *Lübecker Nachrichten* will long remember him as the author of many a local anecdote, vignette and report. Heinz von Eschwege-Lichberg never saw the city on the Spree he so loved again. Under its ruins there also lies a part of his heart. It may indeed be that longing for his old home deprived him of some of the resistance needed to overcome his last illness. . . .' *Lübecker Nachrichten*, 16 March 1951.

mildly: until recently, Herr von Eschwege was completely forgotten. He is not to be found in any directory of writers, there is scarcely a trace of him in any literary archive, and the only work of biographical reference that mentions him shortens his life by twenty years.[3] That is forgivable, because a kind of twilight hovers around his very name. As a writer he called himself Heinz von Lichberg.[4] He was born, however, Heinz von Eschwege. His family background, an ancient line of Hessian aristocrats, was more military than literary. Although his father was a colonel in the infantry,[5] the son took to poetry early on. As a youth Heinz von Lichberg was already placing poems in *Jugend* and *Simplicissimus*. In the middle of the First

---

[3] The Deutsche Bibliothek records his life-span as '1897–1937', an error evidently caused by a confusion with the title *Vier Jahrzehnte Typograph GmbH. 1897–1937*. See *Deutsche Bibliothek*, Normdaten-CD-Rom: Personennamen, Stand: Juli 2003. His actual dates were 1890–1951.

[4] Heinz von Eschwege chose the pseudonym 'Lichberg' as one of the ancient aristocratic names of his family, connected to a hill near the town of Eschwege in Hesse called the 'Leuchtberg'. Family legend had it that the hill was so named because it had once glowed with blood from battlefields around it (I owe this information to Stephan von Eschwege).

[5] Ernst von Eschwege was born in 1858 and died of wounds suffered in the first weeks of the First World War on 4 February 1915 in Cologne. In 1909 he commanded the Third Brandenburger Rifle Battalion in Lübben, in 1911 he served as lieutenant-colonel on the staff of the Graf Kirchbach Regiment in Poznan, and after 1913 as colonel in command of the Fifth Westphalian Infantry Regiment in Cologne. (My thanks to Professor Christian Scheer of Bonn for this information.) Heinz von Eschwege lost his mother when he was seven.

World War, while serving as a lieutenant in the Naval Artillery reserve, he published a collection of fifteen tales, under the title *The Accursed Gioconda*, which appeared in 1916 under the imprint of Falken-Verlag in Darmstadt. Other short books followed.[6] After the war, however, Lichberg mainly devoted himself to journalism, working in Berlin for the newspapers of Scherl-Verlag, the nucleus of the later Hugenberg empire. He became popular in 1929, when he flew as a reporter for Scherl-Verlag on the transatlantic voyage of the Graf Zeppelin; his account of this journey, still obtainable in second-hand book-shops today, was successfully marketed to a proud nation under the title *Zeppelin Goes Round the World*. On this trip Heinz von Lichberg saw New York — over a decade before Vladimir Nabokov.

Tradition has it that the latter came within an inch of committing a historic folly. In the afterword to the novel that made him world-famous and financially independent, Nabokov writes that he was often tempted to destroy the work in gestation:

> Once or twice I was on the point of burning the unfinished draft and had carried my Juanita Dark as far as the shadow of the leaning incinerator on the innocent lawn, when I was

---

[6] *Vom Narrenspiegel der Seele. Gedichte*, Falken-Verlag, Darmstadt 1917. Three years later appeared *Die große Frau. Kleinigkeiten aus dem Leben einiger Menschen*, Schahin Verlag, Darmstadt 1920.

stopped by the thought that the ghost of the destroyed book would haunt my files for the rest of my life.[7]

Juanita Dark was the name Nabokov had then assigned his young heroine. What would have happened if Véra had not restrained her husband from destroying the dangerous bundle of papers? Nabokov would have died a professor of literature and a 'writer's writer'. Google would not spit out millions of entries under a single term. Lolita, Texas, would not have considered applying to change its name. Lolita would not have risen from name to concept.[8] The literature of the twentieth century would have lost one of its most audacious works. And yet there would have been a printed *Lolita* in the world.[9]

---

[7] Vladimir Nabokov, *Lolita*, Penguin Books, New York 1997, p. 312; hereafter *Lolita*.

[8] Lolita has even been called a 'meme', in Richard Dawkins's controversial neologism. 'Every now and again, someone adds a concept to the human meme-pool. Many of these were first postulated in scientific works, but some spring from works of fiction' – among them the pre-pubescent nymphet Lolita. See Sandy Klein, 25 September 2001: http://www.bbc.co.uk/dna/360/A613054.

[9] It even contains the note: 'American copyright by Falken-Verlag, Darmstadt, Germany, 1916'.

SUPPLE GIRLS

A cultivated man of middle age recounts the story of his *coup de foudre*. It all starts when, travelling abroad, he takes a room as a lodger. The moment he sees the daughter of the house, he is lost. She is very young, but her charms instantly enslave him. Heedless of her tender age, he becomes intimate with her. In the end she dies, and the narrator – marked by her for ever – remains alone. The name of the girl supplies the title of the story: '*Lolita*.' It is the ninth of the fifteen tales in the collection *The Accursed Gioconda*, and it appeared forty years before its famous homonym.[10]

---

[10] As late as 1975, you could still buy it for 50 pfenning in a second-hand bookstore in Berlin. In the 1920s and 1930s it must have been quite generally available. Today it is to be found only in a few university libraries. I would like to express my thanks to Herr Rainer Schelling, to whom I owe the first indication of the nymph slumbering in this book.

On reading it today and comparing it with the novel which fortunately was not burnt, a slight feeling of unreality and *déjà-vu* comes over us – as if we had entered one of the labyrinthine stories of Borges. The core of the tale depicts a journey to Spain. The anonymous first-person narrator sets off from South Germany, after bidding farewell to a pair of elderly brothers who own a tavern that he frequents. For reasons that remain unclear, they react strangely to the announcement of his trip. The narrator travels through Paris and Madrid to Alicante, where he takes lodgings in a *pension* by the sea. He plans no more than a quiet holiday. But then, after a brief delay, comes that first fatal glance, which cannot but remind us of the later *Lolita*. There the first-person narrator, Humbert Humbert, makes a journey with the intention of finding a quiet place to work near a lake – surrogate of an Ur-scene by sea. In the little town of Ramsdale he calls on the landlady, Charlotte Haze, whom he finds as unattractive as her residence. Inwardly resolved to leave, he follows Mrs Haze as she conducts him through it:

> I was still walking behind Mrs. Haze through the dining room when, beyond it, there came a sudden burst of greenery – 'the piazza', sang out my leader, and then, without the least warning, a blue sea-wave swelled under my heart and, from a mat in a pool of sun, half-naked, kneeling, turning about on her knees, there was my Riviera love peering at me over dark glasses.
>
> It was the same child – the same frail, honey-hued

shoulders, the same silky supple back, the same chestnut head of hair.[11]

This one glance is enough, and Humbert Humbert stays. So too for Lichberg's first-person narrator, just as the beauty of his young girl also has a dark underside in a mystery of the past:

'The friendly, talkative landlord gave me a room with a wonderful view of the sea, and nothing stood in the way of my enjoying some weeks of undisturbed beauty.

'Until, on the second day, I saw *Lolita*, Severo's daughter.

'By our northern standards she was terribly young, with veiled southern eyes and hair of an unusual reddish gold. Her body was boyishly slim and supple, and her voice full and dark. But there was something more than her beauty that attracted me – there was a strange mystery about her that often troubled me on those moonlit nights.'

Like Humbert, our narrator is immediately bewitched, and abandons any thought of departure. His Lolita too, like Dolores Haze later, is subject to violent changes of mood. Does she want something from him or not; is she hiding secrets in her child's breast? As in the case of the agreeably surprised Humbert Humbert, it is eventually Lolita who seduces the narrator, not the other way round. The author does not say so outright

---

[11] *Lolita*, p. 39.

(we are still in the *Kaiserreich*), but his ellipses and circumlocutions leave the reader in little doubt of the amorous realities:

'There were days when Lolita's big shy eyes regarded me with an unspoken question, and there were evenings when I saw her burst into sudden uncontrollable sobs.

'I had ceased to think of travelling on. I was entranced by the South – and Lolita. Golden hot days and silvery melancholy nights.

'And then came the evening of unforgettable reality and dreamlike magic as Lolita sat on my balcony and sang softly, as she often did. But this time she came to me with halting steps on the landing, the guitar discarded precipitously on the floor. And while her eyes sought out the image of the flickering moon in the water, like a pleading child she flung her trembling little arms around my neck, leant her head on my chest, and began sobbing. There were tears in her eyes, but her sweet mouth was laughing. The miracle had happened. "You are so strong," she whispered.

'Days and nights came and went...'

That is both as inexplicit, and as unambiguous, as befits the period. The days and nights devoted by a lover to the sweet mouth of a lovely nymphet became sexually indecent only with Nabokov, who at first thought of publishing his manuscript anonymously, and later only just escaped the Old Bailey. The correspondence of core plot, narrative perspective, choice of name and title is none the less striking. Unfortunately, as Van

Vladimir Nabokov, aged seven, with his father; the young Heinz von Eschwege.

Veen remarks in *Ada*, there is no logical law that would tell us when a given number of coincidences ceases to be accidental.[12] In its absence, it is not easy to answer – but, of course, even more difficult to dismiss – the unavoidable question: can Vladimir Nabokov, the author of an imperishable *Lolita*, the proud

---

[12] See *Ada or Ardor: A Family Chronicle*; McGraw-Hill, New York 1969, p. 361. Van Veen adds: ' "Tell me", says Osberg's little gitana to the Moors, El Motela and Ramera, "what is the precise minimum of hairs on a body that allows one to call it "hairy"?' We will hear more of Osberg's gipsies later on.

black swan of modern fiction, have known of the ugly duckling that was its precursor? Could he have been affected by it?

The path of the author, at any rate, he could easily have crossed. Heinz von Lichberg lived in the southwest of Berlin, as did Nabokov. As a child, Nabokov had often stopped in Berlin when his family was *en route* to France. A year after the family fled from Russia, in 1919, his parents and siblings moved to the Grunewald district of the city, where Vladimir visited them during his vacations from Trinity College, Cambridge, where he read Slavic and Romance languages. In March 1922 his father, a prominent liberal politician and publicist, was assassinated in the Berlin Philharmonic Theatre by a Russian monarchist. That summer Vladimir moved from England to Berlin, and – he least of anyone would have expected this – stayed there until 1937. In these fifteen Berlin years he got to know Véra Slonim, and married her; became the father of a son; and, under the pen name Sirin, became the outstanding Russian writer of the younger generation. There he wrote no fewer than eight Russian novels, and had almost finished the ninth and greatest, *The Gift*, when he began *The Real Life of Sebastian Knight* and, with it, his conquest of American literature.

None of which yet tells us whether Sirin–Nabokov could even have read the German 'Lolita'. The question, like so many others among Nabokovians, is disputed. So far as his knowledge of matters German went, Nabokov always remained reticent, if not in denial. He let it be understood that, cocooning himself in the Russian exile community for fear of losing his mother tongue, he scarcely spoke any German, and read no German books. His German translator and editor, Dieter E. Zimmer, holds this repeated assertion to be 'objectively somewhat exaggerated, but subjectively the simple truth'.[13] Perhaps subjectively it was true, but objectively somewhat over- (or under-) stated. Nabokov indeed never mastered German – which he had learnt at school[14] – anything like as well as English or French. But he was not lying when he asserted 'a fair knowledge of German' in his application for a Guggenheim Fellowship in 1947.[15] Nor was it an untruth when he wrote to Princeton University Press in 1975 that he read German, but couldn't write in it.[16] Nabokov's antipathy towards the Germans as a people – which later grew into real detestation[17] –

---

[13] Dieter E. Zimmer, *Nabokovs Berlin*, Nicolai Verlag, Berlin 2001, p. 140.

[14] See Brian Boyd, *Nabokov's Pale Fire: The Magic of Artistic Discovery*, Princeton University Press, Princeton 1999, p. 270.

[15] See Schiff, *Véra*, p. 59. Véra, who worked as a secretary and stenographer in Berlin, spoke fluent German; given the close literary communication between the couple, her command of the language should be borne in mind.

[16] Schiff, *Véra*, p. 93 and note.

[17] In February 1944 Nabokov wrote to Mrs Theodore Sherwood: 'I have read with interest the account of your German studies – I liked the bit about Goethe – but the end has puzzled me greatly. I have lived in Germany for 17 years [*sic*] and am quite sure Gretchen has been thoroughly consoled by the secondhand, somewhat blood-stained, but still quite wearable frocks that her soldier friend sent her from the Polish ghettos. No, I am afraid we shall never see the Bernard statue in a German impersonation. It is useless looking at a hyena and hoping that one day domestication or a benevolent gene will turn the creature into a great soft purring tortoiseshell cat.

did not prevent his 'fair knowledge' of their language extending to their letters. Not only was he familiar with the German Romantics and classics.[18] He treasured Hofmannsthal, honoured Kafka, whose translation into English he improved, and despised Thomas Mann (whom he studied with the aid of a dictionary). Of Freud, he remarked that one should read him in the original, which we must therefore presume he had done.[19] The awful first German translation of *Bend Sinister* made him write to the publisher that it would cost him more time and labour to iron out all its howlers than a new translation would

---

Gelding and Mendelism, alas, have their limits. Let us chloroform it – and forget.' *Vladimir Nabokov. Selected Letters 1940–1977*, ed. by Dmitri Nabokov and Matthew J. Bruccoli, Harcourt Brace Jovanovich, San Diego/New York 1989, p. 47. What is remarkable in this letter is less the understandable hatred it expresses than the way Nabokov has adjusted mimetically to the mental patterns of those he hated. A group X is truly and genetically evil, belongs to the animal world, and should be wiped out. It is clear that the writer of such a letter no longer wanted to know – or to have known – much about the language and literature of those hyenas. In October 1945 he wrote to a school-friend living in Palestine: 'Whole Germany must be burnt to ashes several times in a row in order to quench my hatred for it at least slightly, when I am thinking of those perished in Poland.' (Communication of Yuri Leving to the Internet-Forum Nabokv-L [*sic*] of 16 May 2004; the original is in a private collection.)

[18] His book-length commentary on *Evgenii Onegin* alone reveals, time and again, a level of knowledge of them that not every Germanist could display.

[19] For Heine, Goethe, Hofmannsthal, Kafka, Freud, see, *inter alia*, Vladimir Nabokov, *Eigensinnige Ansichten*, ed. Dieter E. Zimmer, Rowohlt Verlag, Reinbek bei Hamburg 2004: *Gesammelte Werke*, vol. XXI, pp 172, 576.

involve.[20] As translator himself, he brought various poems by Heine and the 'dedication' from Goethe's *Faust* into Russian. His opinion of contemporary German literature was low, but plainly not just based on prejudice. In *The Gift* (which also alludes to *Simplicissimus*, where Lichberg had once published poems) he mentions works by Emil Ludwig and the two Zweigs disparagingly, and in one of his stories he took a little side-swipe at Leonhard Frank's novel *Bruder und Schwester* – after, we must hope, having read it.[21]

Someone who knew of Leonhard Frank's incest novel could in principle also have run across a Lolita story by Heinz von Lichberg. Not as a novelist, but as a feuilletonist and travelling reporter for the *Berliner Lokal-Anzeiger*, Lichberg was permanently present during the fifteen years that Nabokov lived in the city. Assuming, then, that by one of those coincidences in which life is richer than any novel should be, the *Gioconda* book fell into his hands: what could have prompted him to leaf through it? A false gleam in its title, perhaps. Lichberg's collection of tales appears to be about Leonardo's *Mona Lisa*. That could have caught the eye of Nabokov, who was an admirer of

---

[20] See *Das Bastardzeichen*, Rowohlt Verlag, *Reinbek bei Hamburg* 1990, *Gesammelte Werke*, vol. VII, p 322. He who can, if necessary, himself repair the blunders in a translation must indeed have at least quite a good knowledge of the target language. Véra later checked the first German translation of *Lolita*, which she found too prudish, preferring – for example – to render 'haunches' as *Gesäß* rather than *Hüften*.

[21] The tale in question was 'The Reunion' (1931). See Zimmer, *Nabokovs Berlin*, p. 140.

Da Vinci. In 1940 Nabokov invoked the shining figure of Leonardo as an example of true human greatness, placing him, as the antithesis of Hitler, on the most glorious of all pedestals.[22] Perhaps in his late twenties or early thirties Nabokov, who might have been interested in the spectacular theft of the *Gioconda* from the Louvre in 1911, picked up a book that promised to reveal her secrets. Lichberg's title story was not in fact about Leonardo's *Gioconda*, but an indifferent figure of the same name. This was something, however, that could be learnt only after opening the book. *If* one did so, the eye might have been caught by the silhouette of a very young girl – assuming that the theme had a certain allure.

---

[22] If Da Vinci were deprived of his sight, he would still be great, whereas if Hitler were deprived of his cannon, he would be a 'mere nonentity'. See Brian Boyd, *The American Years*, Princeton University Press, Princeton 1991, p. 99.

LOLA'S FORMER LIFE

C ould it have aroused a slumbering interest in Nabokov so early on? No doubt this curiosity was already wide awake: there are forerunners of Lolita in his work virtually from the start. In his short story 'A Nursery Tale' (1926), Nabokov had created a child-woman capable of turning the head of the hero. In the company of an old poet – in whom Nabokov retrospectively discovered, to his own astonishment, a prefiguration of Humbert[23] – there sways past Erwin, who spins around to look at her, a child of around fourteen, in a low-cut black cocktail dress:

There was something odd about that face, odd was the flitting glance of her much too shiny eyes, and if she were not just a little girl – the old man's granddaughter, no doubt – one might suspect that her lips were touched up with

[23] See *The Stories of Vladimir Nabokov*, Alfred A. Knopf, New York 1995, p. 644.

rouge. She walked swinging her hips very, very slightly, her legs moved closer together, she was asking her companion something in a ringing voice – and although Erwin gave no command mentally, he knew that his swift secret wish had been fulfilled.[24]

For his secret wishes are fulfilled by no less than the devil. Shining eyes, swinging hips – here, no doubt, is the first of a chain of pre-Lolitas that will henceforward be unbroken. She is still nameless, but already quite the fatal nymphet, as Nabokov would later term her.[25] Next a child-woman leads the wretched

---

[24] *Stories*, p. 170. 'A Nursery Tale' is not the sort of fable the brothers Grimm or Hans Christian Andersen would have dreamt of. Its elegantly handled plot plays with a classic male fantasy. The devil offers to fulfil the timid Erwin's secret erotic dreams. He has a day in which, by mental command, he can select an unlimited number of girls to be his playmates. The only condition is that the sum of those chosen must come to an uneven number. Erwin spends the day in pleasurable recruitment, but spoils it at the last minute by choosing the same girl twice, so shrinking his thirteen elect back to twelve. The object of his fatal mistake is the pre-Lolita.

[25] Brian Boyd, *Vladimir Nabokov. The Russian Years 1899–1940*, Princeton University Press, Princeton 1990, p 259. From the outset, with her first entrance in his work, the nymphet reveals demonic-fantasmagoric traits, to which the young author still unguardedly refers. At the end of the story Erwin is summoned by the devil at midnight to 'Hoffmann Street'. There is no missing Nabokov's allusion: the German Romantic E.T.A. Hoffmann's fantastic tales imperceptibly interweave dream and demonic reality. From this literary signal-mast there runs a silken thread to the German '*Lolita*'. In its very first sentence, Lichberg's tale indicates the model in whose tradition

Albinus of *Laughter in the Dark* to ruin. Not long afterwards appears the first sketch of the plot. He puts it into the mouth of an antipathetic secondary character in *The Gift*, the hero Fyodor's landlord. 'Ah, if only I had a tick or two,' sighs the stepfather of the girl he will love – and the sigh is anything but innocent – 'what a novel I would whip off!':

> Imagine this kind of thing: an old dog – but still in his prime, fiery, thirsting for happiness – gets to know a widow, and she has a daughter, still quite a little girl – you know what I mean – when nothing is formed yet but she has a way of walking that drives you out of your mind – A slip of a girl, very fair, pale with blue under the eyes – and of course she doesn't even look at the old goat. What to do? Well, not long thinking, he ups and marries the widow. Okay. They settle down, the three of them. Here you can go on indefinitely – the temptation, the eternal torment, the itch, the mad hopes. . . .[26]

---

it saw itself: 'Someone threw the name of E.T.A. Hoffmann into the conversation.' The thread should not be overloaded: the most probable time for a (hypothetical) reading of Lichberg by Nabokov is the early 1930s.

[26] *The Gift*, p. 186. Those shadows under the eyes had also made an impression on Lichberg's narrator. In *The Gift*, the landlord has not just stumbled on this Dostoevskyan story; it is his own. He has made approaches to the young Zina; his marriage is a failure; perhaps he only married the mother to be around the daughter.

And here Nabokov did go on, writing five years later in Paris a short novel, *The Enchanter*, in which the germ cell of *Lolita* has already developed into a full embryo – certainly the most *osé* version of all. Ten years after that, he began the composition of the novel which, despite every temptation of the incinerator, he triumphantly completed in Ithaca in December 1953.

It is noticeable, however, that Lolita, although she emerges so early as a figure and a theme, as a name appears very late. Nabokov told *Lolita*'s first commentarist, Alfred Appel Jr, that he had originally intended to call his heroine Virginia and the novel *Ginny*.[27] In the manuscript she bore the name Juanita Dark for a long time. It was only later that Nabokov discovered a thousand reasons why the name Lolita, with which the novel begins and ends, had become essential.[28] This fact alone might

---

[27] See *The Annotated Lolita, Edited, with Preface, Introduction and Notes by Alfred Appel, Jr*, Vintage, New York 1991, p. 358; hereafter Appel.

[28] In the foreword to the novel, the fictive John Ray explains that he has altered the surname 'Haze', but the first name was 'too closely interwound with the inmost fibre of the book to allow one to alter it': *Lolita*, p. 4. In his *Playboy* interview Nabokov declared: 'For my nymphet I needed a diminutive with a lyrical lilt to it. One of the most limpid and luminous letters is "L". The suffix "-ita" has a lot of Latin tenderness, and this I required too. Hence: Lolita.' *Strong Opinions*, Vintage, New York 1990, p. 25. There was another external reason for the name to be remembered: 'Dolores', as the baptismal name from which Lola-Lolita is derived, was also the toponym of the town in Colorado near which Nabokov caught the first female specimen of *Lycaeides sublivens Nabokov*: see Appel, p 333. Still, we get from Dolores to Lolita only if we already know the latter; and we do not get to Lolita via considerations on the lyricism of the letter L. Maurice

suggest that he was not conscious of any predecessor to his nymphet, since if he had wanted to cover his tracks he would surely have done just the opposite – unless, of course, he precisely did not want to cover them.

In both cases Lolita is a diminutive form of Lola – in the one of Spanish and in the other of Mexican origin.[29] Interestingly, there is also, as Appel noted, a German strain in Nabokov's Lola. The *femme fatale* of that name in Sternberg's movie *The Blue Angel* was played by Marlene Dietrich, to whom Humbert once compares Lolita's mother.[30] On parting, he evens calls her Marlene, another time Lotte; while her surname, Haze, is close to the German *Hase* (Bunny), as Nabokov confided – perhaps

---

Couturier, the editor of the Pléiade edition of Nabokov, points to two French texts in which the name Lolita likewise appears: *En villégiature. Lolita*, by Isidore Gès (1894) and *La Chanson de Lolita*, by René Riche (1920), related to Pierre Louys's nymph-celebrating *Chanson de Bilitis* (1894). An astounding anticipation of Humbert's opening passage can also be found in Valéry Larbaud's *Des prénoms féminins* (1927), where the names Dolores, Lola and Lolita are declined in their specific connotations. (Communication of 2 April 2004 to the Nabokov-Forum Nabokv-L.)

[29] Charlotte Haze spent her honeymoon in Mexico, hence Lolita's name. For the white, Protestant middle class of 1935 the choice of name remains unusual. This was also the view of Charles Kinbote, who annotated John Shade's lines 'It was a year of tempests. Hurricane/Lolita swept from Florida to Maine' with the comment: 'Why our poet chose to give his 1958 hurricane a little-used Spanish name (sometimes given to parrots) instead of Linda or Lois, is not clear': Vladimir Nabokov, *Pale Fire*, Vintage Books, New York 1989, pp. 49, 191.

[30] See Appel, p 332; *Lolita*, p. 37.

merely to flatter the magazine – to an interviewer from *Play-boy*.[31] That Humbert once calls his Lolita *die Kleine*, and can pity her for a 'rustic German' look, belongs to the same astoundingly consistent background.[32]

The figure herself bears as much resemblance to her Hispano-German forerunner as one young girl may bear to another. They are in no way twins, and the likeness between them is fleeting – as fleeting as the scent of Spanish toilet powder that wafts from Humbert's first love.[33] The name Humbert gives this girl, taken early by death, offers another scent. He calls her Annabel, after Edgar Allan Poe's poem of the same name on the dead child-bride Annabel Lee. Humbert's unfulfilled passion for Annabel leads him into the arms of Lolita, who seems to him a reincarnation of this first nymphet. The very names of his two loves – 'Annabel Haze, alias Dolores Lee, alias Loleeta'[34] – blend and merge into one another.

Such fusion is a process found early in Nabokov's work. Lolita has another and largely unknown predecessor called Annabella, a character in his play *The Waltz Invention*. The plot of this drama, which dates from 1938, is very close to the earlier 'Nursery Tale'. Through a set of fantastic circumstances

---

[31] *Strong Opinions*, p. 25.

[32] *Lolita*, pp. 135, 180.

[33] Ibid., p. 15. A Spanish aroma also, of course, surrounds Mérimée's Carmen, often evoked by Humbert. In *Ada* Lolita appears as an 'Andalusian gypsy' (cf. Appel, pp. 328, 358 and below).

[34] *Lolita*, p. 167.

Waltz, its inhibited, demented hero, finds himself in a position to fulfil his erotic dreams. Lord of the world, he lets a harem be assembled for him, but rejects every woman he is offered in favour of Annabella. Although she is five years older than Lolita – Nabokov took care to specify the difference in a postwar afterword – 'little Annabella' is 'a very young girl', 'less than a child', but thoroughly eroticized by a series of ambiguities and *risqué* allusions.[35] The lovesick Waltz is so smitten with her that he threatens to blow up the whole country if her father does not deliver her to him.

Nabokov's play, though certainly no masterpiece, is carefully constructed. It seems all the more striking that he inserts into it a character who is a pure name, never appears on stage, has no function and is mentioned only once: an old, grey-bearded relative of the hero, supposedly the genius in the background, to whose imaginary invention the play owes its title. He is a cousin of the same name.

In Nabokov's Annabella-drama there is thus an ominous male pair by the name of Waltz.[36] In German, where it originates,

---

[35] Annabella enjoys sunning herself, like Lolita; there are male jokes about her talent at riding (p. 17); she is called a 'tactless virgin' and 'the hussy!' (p. 70); 'a promised kiss' emerges: 'open mouth and closed eyes' (p. 70).

[36] The invention of the infernal machine that gives its title to the play 'is the work of a cousin of mine, a grey bearded man, also called Waltz, Walter Waltz, Walt Waltz, a genius, a super-genius!'. The name Walzer appears, of course, in the Russian original as Vals and in the American as Waltz. *Izobretenie Val'sa* was published in November 1938 in the Russian exile journal *Russkie zapiski*. Dmitri Nabokov translated his father's last play in

the word for waltz is Walzer. The reader may well ask what the brothers in Lichberg's *Lolita* are called. Here is perhaps the most striking of all the concordances between the two texts. Their name, too, is Walzer. Even the grey beard – in Lichberg streaked with red – recurs in Nabokov.

1966 under the title *The Waltz Invention* (Phaedra, New York 1966). On both occasions the double meaning of the name, as also the term for the German dance, was preserved. 'The name is only good for a dance', says the Minister as he listens to Waltz. In his later English foreword Nabokov underlined the *double entendre* of the title, 'which means not only the invention of Vals (or Valse), but also "the invention of the waltz."'

LOLITA AS DEMON; THE SPANISH FRIEND

The subtitle of *The Accursed Gioconda* describes the stories collected in it as 'grotesques', which fits *Lolita* only partially. The tale is in fact a ghost story *à la* Hoffmann, whose theme, introduced in the first sentence, determines both outer and inner narratives. During a conversation among guests at the house of one Countess Beate, talk turns to the relations between art and reality: a conventional opening whose function is to introduce an inner plot.[37] The lady of the house draws the young writer among her guests into

[37] A device from which the young Nabokov himself did not always abstain, as the beginning of 'The Passenger', a tale of 1927 – Nabokov was then three years older than Lichberg when he wrote *The Accursed Gioconda* – shows: ' "Yes, Life is more talented than we", sighed the writer, tapping the cardboard mouthpiece of his Russian cigarette against the lid of his case. "The plots Life thinks up now and then! How can we compete with that goddess? Her works are untranslatable, indescribable." "Copyright by the author", suggested the critic, smiling . . .': *The Stories of Vladimir Nabokov*, p. 183.

a discussion. After half a page, a hitherto silent professor cuts in. He wishes to recount something that has burdened his mind for years – something that could be experience or fantasy, he still does not know which. So begins the real narrative: a highly Hoffmannesque story, whose core encapsulates the very theme which germinated in Nabokov's fiction from the 1920s onwards.

The narrator is a student in a South German university town who frequents the tavern run by the Walzer brothers. Lichberg already scatters some small hints of a Spanish background. On an armchair lies a black silk headscarf, 'of the sort Spanish girls wear on days of celebration'.[38] It occurs to him that something odd may be going on in this place, which seems to be open only for him, but he wastes no further thought on it. One night, passing by the tavern, he hears angry, youthfully transformed voices, a violent quarrel and a terror-stricken cry from a woman's throat. But the next morning everything at the brothers' establishment seems so unchanged that he doubts his experience and is ashamed to ask them about it. Soon afterwards he sets off on the trip to Spain whose announcement so agitates the brothers. Lichberg has thus prepared everything for a finale in which the mystery's solution will be revealed. It lies in a picture. In the *pension* in Alicante hangs a drawing that seems to depict Lolita. The impression, however, is deceptive. It is Lola, the grandmother of Lolita's great-grandmother, 'who

---

[38] Ada also wears such a Spanish shawl, which certainly goes with the airy black skirt called a lolita in the novel: *Ada* pp. 77, 488–9.

was strangled by her lovers after a quarrel a hundred years ago!'.

Here is the solution to the mystery, and the crux of Lichberg's plot. Lolita is not just any enchanting young girl. She is under a curse, and a demonic repetition compulsion. The narrator learns of this haunted background, once he finally – now in fear of Lolita's dangerous love – decides to leave. Lolita's father explains to him what has happened since the Ur-Lola drove her lovers mad, and paid for it by being murdered. Since then the women of the line would always have just one daughter, and then die insane a few weeks after the birth of their child. He predicts the death of his own daughter, and on the same evening the narrator finds a small red flower on his pillow.

> 'Lolita's farewell gift, I thought to myself, and took it in my hand. Then I saw that it was really white, and red only with Lolita's blood.
>
> 'That was the way she loved.'

The blood-drenched blossom in a bed, given as a love-token, seems to be a classic symbol of deflowering, if not of demonic nymphet-love in general, even if the author, later explaining that the blood is from a cut on Lolita's arm, perhaps really had only a flower in mind.[39] It is in any case a farewell. That night

---

[39] Humbert Humbert, *par contre*, has no blossom in mind when he recounts his first night with Lolita and inquires rhetorically of his jurors: 'Did I

her father's prophecy is fulfilled.[40] Towards midnight the narrator is visited by a vivid dream. He is witness to a phantasmagoric scene of murder, as he sees the Ur-Lola – 'or was it indeed Lolita?' – driving two lovers into a white heat and finally being strangled by them. In the murderers he recognizes the twins Aloys and Anton Walzer. The next morning he discovers that Lolita has died during the night.

> 'My beloved little Lolita lay in her small, narrow bed with her eyes wide open. Her teeth were clenched convulsively in her lower lip, and her fragrant blonde hair lay tangled.'

The diminutives underline once again that this is no woman, but a child, of whom the narrator takes leave with a broken heart. If he takes Lolita's soul with him, in the words of the tale, this is an ambiguous consolation that implies he might not escape her.

Curse, demonism, repetition compulsion: these are under-

---

deprive her of her flower?' (*Lolita*, p. 135) There is an obscene variant of the bloody flower in the scene of Humbert's last evening with Lolita before her illness and flight: 'I undressed her. . . . Her brown rose tasted of blood' (p. 240).

[40] As had been an earlier dream of the narrator, in which he foresees, while still in South Germany, the *pension* in Alicante. This micro-theme, too, would have greatly interested Nabokov. Prophetic or synchronic dreams are a theme he repeatedly wove into his fiction, and sought to research in life with the same seriousness as J.W. Dunne, whose *Experiment with Time* he took as an example in keeping a dream diary.

currents in the other *Lolita* too. Nabokov's child-woman is also a revenant, the reincarnation of an earlier, fatal *gamine sans merci*. Annabel, his first love by the sea, burns desire for nymphets for ever into Humbert. She puts him under a spell that he can escape only by allowing her to rise again in Lolita.[41] Nabokov's novel, one could say, is about not paedophilia, but demonism. Humbert is under an erotic-demonic compulsion. Thirty years earlier, in Nabokov's 'Nursery Tale', it was the devil who supplied the earliest, still nameless Lolita to the hero. That has not changed in the *chef d'œuvre*. According to Humbert's caustic complaint, it is the devil himself who leads him on and makes a fool of him, who charms him with Lolita and then whisks her away from under his nose, and who must eventually give him some respite, if he wants to keep Humbert a while longer as a plaything.[42] Humbert knows very well under whose spell he has fallen:

> Now I wish to introduce the following idea. Between the age limits of nine and fourteen there occur maidens who, to certain bewitched travellers, twice or many times older than they, reveal their true nature, which is not human, but nymphic (that is, demoniac).

---

[41] Appel is right to call *Lolita* a book 'about the spell exerted by the past' (Appel, p. xxiii). The mythic succession of Lolas–Lolitas projected by Heinz von Lichberg also lurks in Humbert's thoughts, as he imagines Lolita's granddaughter, Lolita the Third, as a future playmate: *Lolita*, p. 174.

[42] *Lolita*, pp. 55–6.

Lolita is the 'immortal daemon disguised as a female child'.[43] The same is true of the Lolita of 1916. She too is half demon, half victim of a curse, and, like her lover, under the compulsion of the past.[44] What compulsively repeats itself over the years always ends by exploding in violence. It is not only Lichberg's tale that leads into the dream-like scene of a dramatic, grotesque murder. The finale of Nabokov's novel is also a dream-like, phantasmagoric killing.[45] Humbert and Clare Quilty, the two lovers of Lolita, intermingle in this scene, becoming the twins they were from the start in Lichberg. Lolita's seducer, Quilty, is Humbert's dark shadow and second self. In their tussle they lose even their grammatical identities:

> We rolled all over the floor in each other's arms, like two huge helpless children. He was naked and goatish under his robe, and I felt suffocated as he rolled over me. I rolled over

---

[43] Ibid., pp. 16, 139.

[44] In Lichberg there is even a precise time-span for the working of the spell. When the narrator parts from Lolita, she bites him in the hand with all the strength of her little mouth. 'These scars of love', confesses the casualty to his listeners, 'have remained indelible even twenty-five years later.' We encounter the same interval when Humbert, in a shock of anagnorisis, sees Lolita for the first time – his re-embodied first love, from whose spell he has never escaped: 'The twenty-five years I have lived since then, tapered to a palpitating point, and vanished.'

[45] Nabokov confirmed the unreal, oneiric character of Humbert's murder scene privately, in a letter that speaks of its 'dream-distortion': *Selected Letters*, p. 408.

him. We rolled over me. They rolled over him. We rolled over us.[46]

Finally Humbert succeeds in killing his *alter ego* – no easy task, since the bullets in Quilty's body, instead of destroying him, seem to jab him with fresh energy. With the death of the billy goat, his own fate is sealed. A few weeks later Humbert too, the tragic satyr, is a dead man.

In Lichberg's tale, it is not the rival but the woman who is murdered. Nabokov time and again plays with this variant too. Not only does a leitmotiv of quotations from *Carmen*, suggesting that the betrayed lover may finally shoot his faithless beloved, tempt his reader along this false track to the very end. Even at his farewell to Lolita, Humbert flirts with the image of drawing his revolver and doing something stupid.[47] As we know, the pregnant Lolita is spared this end. Indirectly, however, the curse still seems to radiate from the *Gioconda*. Lichberg's Lola is murdered shortly after the death of her daughter. Nabokov's Lolita dies in the weeks following childbirth, having given issue to a stillborn girl.

Each time, though, the last word belongs not to death but to art. Lolita and her history, sticky with marrow and blood and beautiful bright-green flies, make Humbert into a writer. The

---

[46] *Lolita*, p. 297.

[47] 'Then I pulled out my automatic – I mean, this is the kind of fool thing a reader might suppose I did. It never even occurred to me to do it': *Lolita*, p. 280.

novel ends with his hope of the only refuge that he and his muse can find together: 'I am thinking of aurochs and angels, the secret of durable pigments, prophetic sonnets, the refuge of art. And this is the only immortality you and I may share, my Lolita.'

The great novel's famous ending: he who survives Lolita becomes through her an artist. The tale of 1916 ends not very differently. The professor, too, is initiated into art by Lolita. When he has finished his story, the countess – who has been listening to him with closed eyes – murmurs: 'You are a poet'.

Might immortality smile on his Lolita too? Her only chance would be a hide-out in Nabokov's novel. Not so small a chance in this majestic structure undermined by so many caverns and secret corridors. Appel's commentary needs 140 closely printed pages to decipher only the most important allusions. The name Heinz von Lichberg, of course, does not occur in it. Still, there is a passage in which a tender *mise en abîme* appears to be concealed. Humbert watches Lolita in a circle of other nymphets by the swimming-pool, and recalls:

> ... today, putting my hand on my ailing heart, I really do not think any of them ever surpassed her in desirability, or if they did, it was so two or three times at the most, in a certain light, with certain perfumes blended in the air – once in the hopeless case of a pale Spanish child, the daughter of a heavy-jawed nobleman, and another time – *mais je divague*.

Why does Nabokov introduce this Spanish daughter of a

nobleman – not the daughter of a Spanish nobleman, be it noted? No obvious function attaches to her. In the following pages she reappears inconspicuously as Lolita's little Spanish friend. She is the 'lesser nymphet, a diaphanous darling', who skips with Lolita. Taking his leave, Humbert flashes a smile to 'the shy, dark-haired page girl of my princess'.[48] But who is smiling at whom here – Humbert at a missed chance, or his creator, with a tint to her hair, at the lesser Spanish nymphet of the aristocrat Von Lichberg? If Nabokov had wanted to hide a small thanks for certain page services, he certainly couldn't have done so more elegantly.

---

[48] *Lolita*, pp. 161, 163–4.

LITTLE LOTTE AND THE FÜHRER

Back from blood-clotted art to no less bloody life. On 30 January 1933 Hitler was nominated Reichskanzler. This was the day the Nazis seized power. That evening, a nationwide broadcast hailed the torch-lit procession to the Reichskanzlei with an elated commentary. The two radio reporters looked out at the SA marching past, and 'the vast masses of the people cheering the Führer'. Then they turned their gaze towards the Reichskanzlei. There stood Adolf Hitler:

> with a deadly stern face at the window, he has just been torn away from his work, there is no trace of triumph in his expression, or anything like it, just the serious look of labour. He has been interrupted. Yet there is a light in his eyes at this awakening of Germany, these masses of people from all walks of life, from all strata of the population, who are marching past beneath him, workers of head and hand, all class differences effaced.

The recording can be heard in every documentary of the time: the enthusiastic voice still rings in the ear. It is the voice of Heinz von Lichberg.[49] The creator of the first *Lolita* joined the Nazi Party in May 1933. Soon afterwards he became a member of the editorial board of the *Völkische Beobachter*. But the next year it became clear that politically he was not entirely reliable. In February 1934, the 'strange cultural-political activity of Herr Lichberg-Eschwege' was attacked in a sharp letter of protest to the editorial board. Lichberg, writing as a dramatic critic, had panned a Nazi play in the official organ of the Party. The Berlin Gauleitung, the writer indignantly pointed out, had distributed several hundred tickets for the première to Party members, and the *Völkische Beobachter* had trampled it into the ground! In general, the recent theatre criticism of Herr von Lichberg had met with the utmost rejection from Party comrades in Berlin.[50]

Perhaps they never liked this elegant apparition. From the start, a touch of the dandy and of the cosmopolitan may have not suited Party militants. Von Lichberg is represented as the very type of an immaculately clad, slightly melancholy sportsman aristocrat of the old school; now come down in the world, but withal a marvellous rider, a guest at the captain's table on

---

[49] The other reporter of this historic experience was the SA-Sturmführer Wulf Bley, http://www.swr.de/zeitenwende/galerie/moments/1930-1939.html: *Moments of History. Eine Komposition der Erinnerung.* http://www.jacobasch.de/artike17.htm: *75 Jahre deutscher Rundfunk.*

[50] Letter of 1 February 1934 to the editorial board of the *Völkische Beobachter*, for the attention of retired Captain Weiss; original in Bundesarchiv.

(Right) Heinz von Lichberg in military uniform, 'yet preserving an air of the solitary poet about him, a type not so utterly different from the young Vladimir himself'. (Left) Nabokov in 1919, an undergraduate at Trinity College, Cambridge.

transatlantic crossings, a charmer on the dance-floor, yet preserving an air of the solitary poet about him. This type was, by the way, not so utterly distant from the young Vladimir himself.

Despite the attack on him, Lichberg remained on the mast of the *Völkische Beobachter* while continuing to write light-weight feuilletons for the *Berliner Lokal-Anzeiger*. Over time he obviously wearied of these. In 1933 he was already complaining to Hans Grimm that he had become a journalistic slave to Scherl-Verlag, with which he had for years now been at odds.[51]

---

[51] A brief exchange of letters between Lichberg and Grimm, author of the notorious novel *Volk ohne Raum* and later President of the Writers' Asso-

In 1935 he tried once more to establish himself as an author, publishing a novel entitled *Nantucket-Lightship*. Set in New York, the book sketches a portrait of the city in the Prohibition era, rich in details obviously derived from personal experience, and equally rich in racist clichés.[52] Apart from a Festschrift two

---

ciation under the Third Reich, together with whom he had served in the Naval Artillery during the First World War, is preserved in literary archives at Marbach. Von Eschwege was a direct descendant of the Grimm brothers (his father, Ernst, was a grandson of the painter Ludwig Emil Grimm), but he was not related to Hans Grimm.

[52] For just a small impression: Von Lichberg's first-person narrator, Peter Andresen, walks through the streets of the Jewish district. 'Against the doors of the dirty shops leant Hebrews, old men with ringlets – one grabbed at my sleeve, wanted to take me inside and blabber something at me. Scarcely had I freed myself from him than the next one seized on me, a young grinning Galician with gold incisors and a greasy tie. I looked at his grubby hands, sausage-like fingers with their torn, blackened nails. I did not really want him to clean his filthy fingers on the sleeve of my light-coloured suit. "Let go!" I said. He grinned still more pressingly. His mouth widened from one ear to the another. Two of his upper right molars were missing, only blackish stumps were to be seen. But his eyes became sad. He did not let go. A waterfall of words, and a repulsive sort of smell, flowed from his mouth. "Let go!" I said. "Immediately!" He squinted quickly at my hands, and when he saw my fists, released me. But when I took a step further, he unleashed a flood of venomous curses at me. Out of every door men like him immediately appeared' (*Nantucket-Feuerschiff*, Scherl-Verlag, Berlin 1935, p. 92). Elsewhere a certain Carsten, who has moved to New York and is praised for his decency by the narrator, confesses his nostalgia for Germany: 'I would really like to go back, if I had the wherewithal to do so. Here nothing's happening any more. There will be one crash after another

years later, no further publications materialized. In 1937, the same year that Nabokov left Germany, Heinz von Lichberg bade farewell to his readers.

On 19 December 1937 a last article by him appeared in the *Berliner Lokal-Anzeiger*, whose editor had asked contributors to fill out a wish-list for Christmas. The sharpness of Lichberg's response was only thinly veiled. He respected the inquiry, of course, but it betrayed a lot of benignly childish optimism:

You see – we human beings all run around with dream-wishes locked up in the most secret chamber of our hearts, which no one will type out for you in double spacing. Or do you think that anyone will tell you that he is inwardly gnawed by longing for a particular little Lotte or Anna?

---

and then everything will go bust. The good times are over. The big-shots are in the saddle and are completely wrecking the country. There's nothing but bribery, blood-sucking, intrigue. All that flourishes are artificial flowers. What we need here is a very strong man – if *one* here were even enough – to put all the stockjobbers and the rest of the rabble against the wall.' Andresen replies: 'Whom are you talking to? What we need in Germany is the same strong man – though we have to struggle not only against the riff-raff in our own country, but the crazy arrogance of our enemies abroad. When one just thinks of disarmament and Versailles –' (ibid., p. 135). This is supposed to be said in 1930, and so, apart from anything else, has the *haut-goût* of prophecy after the event; by 1935 the strong man was in power and the firing squads were at work. In 1934 even a close relative of Lichberg had fallen victim to the regime: Von Papen's press spokesman Herbert von Bose, who was betrayed in his attempt to get Hindenburg to oust Hitler from his post as Chancellor of the Reich.

Even if we banish from our thoughts the name-games Nabokov will play with Lotte, Lolita and Lottelita,[53] this secret, nagging longing for *little Lotte* gives the valediction an almost symbolic force. Heinz von Lichberg withdraws from the public sphere, and returns to the military world. There he makes a career in the Wehrmacht – or, more precisely, in the secret services. The signs are that this worldly, well-travelled journalist was recruited into the circle around Admiral Canaris, head of foreign intelligence under the Third Reich.[54] At first Lichberg appears to have been assigned to work in the propaganda department of the Second Section of the Abwehr.[55] By 1941 he was in the High Command of Army Group C (North), and a year later – now a Lieutenant-Colonel – he served in the Abwehr Command 204. In 1943 he was ordered to Leszno, for duties with the secret military police of the Abwehr in Poland. What he did or saw there we can only speculate: the records

---

[53] *Lolita*, p. 76.

[54] An indication is that Lichberg's membership of the NSDAP lapsed on 23 June 1938; this was customary on transfer to service in the Wehrmacht, where officers could not be Party members. Canaris had created Abteilung II of the Abwehr just three weeks earlier. This section – responsible for sabotage, provocation, liaison with Volkdeutsche groups, and propaganda – was headed by Colonel Helmut Groscurth.

[55] In Groscurth's service diary, the entry for 5 December 1939 notes: 'Conversation with Major von Xylander and Captain von Eschwege about propaganda against North Africans', presumably in the detachments of the French Army: *Tagebücher eines Abwehroffiziers 1939–1940* (ed. Helmut Krausnick and Harold Deutsch), p. 314.

Nabokov in the Grand Rue, Montreux; Von Lichberg, Lt-Colonel (rtd) and Writer.

are thin. The following year, in February 1944, he was sent on missions unknown to Paris – the city Nabokov had fled four years before, as German troops approached. When hostilities ended, Lichberg was a British prisoner of war.[56] Released in April 1946, he moved to Lübeck, where – 'Lieutenant-Colonel (rtd) and Writer', as styled in the German *Debrett* – he died without issue in March 1951. A branch of the Von Eschwege family came to an end with the author of the first *Lolita*.

---

[56] Service data kindly supplied by the Deutsche Dienststelle (WASt), Berlin.

Heinz von Lichberg's wife survived her husband by a dozen years, dying in Neuwied in 1963.[57] It is curious to think that, as the hurricane of *Lolita* swept the United States and then raced back towards Europe, it might have awakened in Lichberg's widow a faint recollection of the youthful work of her husband. *Lolita* . . . didn't that ring a bell?

---

[57] My thanks for this information to Jürgen von Bose. Martha (Tilly) Küster, born in Charlottenburg, Berlin, married Heinz von Eschwege in 1921. See *Genealogisches Handbuch des Adels. Adelige Häuser A*, Limburg an der Lahn 1960, vol. iv, p. 344.

THREE POSSIBILITIES;
GROWING DANGER

And there remains the insistent question: would it have *rightly* rung a bell? What exactly are we dealing with here? Plainly, there are only three possibilities, at any rate until someone shows us a fourth.[58] Let us consider each in turn.

The first is that Nabokov was completely unaware of Lichberg's tale, and we are in the presence of one of those fortuitous coincidences which recur in the history of art and

---

[58] The possibility of some oral report of the book to Nabokov, raised by Marcel Reich-Ranicki in *Der Spiegel*, is not very plausible (still less the grounds advanced for it, which betray a certain *déformation professionelle*, namely the idea that on his arrival in Berlin Nabokov's German was not good enough to read it – forgetting that non-reviewers can even read books that are ten or twenty years old). If someone had merely recounted the story to Nabokov, they would certainly not have entered into its details, would have ignored the names in it, and would have been unlikely to single out the nymphet as its core theme. To register the latter, which can be overlooked, a sensibility like that at work in 'A Nursery Tale' was required.

science. As we have known since Aristotle, it is inherent to the laws of probability that the improbable occurs. Paradoxically, it even occurs more frequently than we would intuitively suppose. Littlewood's Law, called after the Cambridge mathematician, states that on average everyone can expect one wonder a month, which only goes to show that in the world of statistics, guesses based on common sense are likely to be too conservative. Why, then, should the chain of concordances between the two *Lolitas*, instead of being anchored in a *fundamentum in re*, not simply dangle from the ether of pure contingency? Why should it not simply be a splendid, mysterious, even faintly comical example of the way life displays patterns that look deliberate yet are only the caprices of coincidence? In a certain sense this would be a classic Nabokovian theme.

And, of course, nothing can be excluded. Still, by the beards of the prophets, or of the Walzer brothers: even granted the counterintuitive aspects of probability, how likely is it that two authors would independently baptize a male couple with the same unusual surname? How likely is it that they would further create, again independently of each other, a child-woman called Lolita, and have her seduce a guest in a boarding-house? How likely that they would send, again in perfect independence of each other, the inventor of a futuristic weapon into the antechamber of the War Department? (But we anticipate.) That Nabokov should at some point in his time in Berlin have read a book in German seems, to put it moderately, somewhat less improbable.

The second possibility takes us deep into the hypothetical.[59] It runs like this. Nabokov could have come upon Lichberg's *Accursed Gioconda*, and found in it a theme that had already begun to take shape in his mind. Thereafter he forgot the tale. Later, drawn to the surface by new bait, whole fragments of the Ur-*Lolita* rose from the depths. Nabokov remained quite unconscious of this resurgence of memory in what seemed to him to be entirely his own creation. The history of literature is not without examples of this phenomenon, called cryptomnesia.[60] Nabokov himself must have been familiar with it:

---

[59] In earlier articles, the enumeration of possibilities above differed – the second and third being explored in reverse order from that here. Through constant sifting of further grains of rice – that is, small, hard beads of evidence – the balance of the argument almost imperceptibly shifted.

[60] In the very nature of things, cryptomnesia is hard to prove after the event and still harder to refute, so arguments appealing to it do not meet an important Popperian test. The world would be simpler if it permitted only phenomena that fitted snugly into falsifiable theories; unfortunately, not all phenomena take the trouble to do so. Cryptomnesia is seldom retrospectively provable, but the Musil scholar Karl Corino has recently given us an attested example. After a third reading of Jacobsen's *Niels Lyhne*, Robert Musil came upon a passage in his own *Man Without Qualities*, a conversation between Ulrich and Agathe, that was plainly influenced by the work of his Danish colleague. 'Rereading *Niels Lyhne*, Musil had completely forgotten the plot, but on a closer analysis was forced to acknowledge that an analogous situation in the Danish novel "had served him as a model", without him being aware of it. "So if we exclude a coincidence, we might say that some twenty years later this memory worked its effect", commented Musil in his diary.' See Karl Corino, 'Die doppelte Lolita'. In Thomas Mann's

according to his own account, he often read two or three books a day, which he immediately forgot.[61] And with him, of course, as with any author, a part of what was written went back to what was read.

The advantage of this variant is that it does not overwork coincidence, and spares us other difficult questions. For how could an author who was so uncommonly proud of conjuring the fictional world out of nothing have at the last moment changed the name Juanita to Lolita, if he was aware that he would be citing an unworthy predecessor? The question and the problem do not apply if he was unaware of it. The disadvantage of this hypothesis is that it is hard to square with the details of the third possibility.

The third hypothesis is this: Nabokov indeed knew Lichberg's tale – from 1933 onwards at the latest – and, half-inserting, half-blurring its traces, set himself to that art of quotation which Thomas Mann, himself a master of it, called 'higher cribbing'.[62] The stress lies on 'higher'. Of course, this possibility would have as little to do with plagiarism as it did in the case of Mann, who was quite self-conscious about what was he was doing, saying, with Molière, 'Je prends mon bien où je

---

diaries there are similar scenes of re-recognition. That rediscovery of what was forgotten is itself typically a matter of chance makes proof of cryptomnesia in general all the more difficult.

[61] *Eigensinnige Ansichten*, p. 46.

[62] There are, of course, mixed forms. At point in time A, Nabokov could have been conscious of source X that had trickled away by a later point, B.

le trouve'. Who would deny him or any other great author this right? Literature has always been a huge crucible, in which familiar themes are continually recast; Nabokov would have been the only author to escape this process – the first whose work was sheer material, not what a great writer made of it. Nothing of what we admire in the novel *Lolita* is already to be found in the tale; the former is in no way deducible from the latter.[63] All of this needs no further explanation; it is self-evident to anyone who can read. Still: did Nabokov consciously borrow and quote?

Much suggests that he did, once we take a small step backwards and look not just at the two girls, but at the works in which they are framed. For nowhere is it written that Nabokov could have reacted to Lichberg's *Lolita* only in his novel of the same name. And no one can prescribe that he should have read only one of the fifteen tales in *The Accursed Gioconda*.

One of the most remarkable scenes in Lichberg's *Lolita* is the magical competition to which the brothers Walzer are challenged by an imperiously mocking Lola:

---

[63] A nice résumé of what is to be found only in *Lolita* and in no preceding work is offered, together with a possible source in Bunin, by Tom Bolt in a letter to the Nabokv-L forum of 26 May 2004. Whatever the similarities of plot, in Bunin there is 'no Quilty and no Catullus, no Aztec red convertible, no McFate, no Blue Licks obelisk, no Kasbeam barber, no sign of the Tigermoth, no small matter-of-fact voice, no big pink bubble with juvenile connotations, no lovely, trustful, dreamy, enormous country'.

' "*I will love the one who is strongest!*" ',

'So they took off their jackets and their muscles swelled. But they realized they were equally strong.

' "*I will love the one who is tallest!*" ' Her eyes flashed.

'And lo and behold, the men grew taller and taller, their necks lengthened and grew thinner, and their sleeves burst right through to their elbows. Their faces became ugly and distorted, and I thought I could hear their bones cracking. But not by so much as a hair did one become larger than the other.'

And lo and behold, just this grotesque scene was elaborated by Nabokov in a story he wrote in 1933. Here too there is a pair of brothers, metaphorically even 'identical twins',[64] who suddenly begin to grow larger, and here too one of them is called Anton. The brothers threaten their new neighbour, after whom the story is called: an *émigré* who is harassed and finally murdered by these brutalized German philistines.[65] As the story begins,

---

[64] 'The red sweater and grey went up to the window and actually leant out, becoming identical twins': *The Stories of Vladimir Nabokov*, p. 357.

[65] 'The New Neighbour' is a forerunner of the 1937 tale 'Cloud, Castle, Lake', in which a shy Russian exile is tormented by a group of German travellers and – one possible reading – driven to suicide. The twist in the earlier tale is the false lead that Nabokov lays, letting the reader believe that the dreamy night owl Romantkowski is a writer, perhaps a novelist, in any case not the *leonardo* – that is, counterfeiter – that the English title of the story already betrays him to be. The now suggestive association Leonardo–Gioconda was not yet possible in 1933; Nabokov first encountered the slang

the brothers visit the new tenant in his apartment. He obscurely senses the danger they represent, his thoughts wander, and like his predecessor, Lichberg's narrator in Alicante, he slips into a day dream or vision:

> Meanwhile the brothers began to swell, to grow, they filled up the whole room, the whole house, and then grew out of it . . . Gigantic, imperiously reeking of sweat and beer, with beefy voices and senseless speeches, with fecal matter replacing the human brain, they provoke a tremor of ignoble fear. I don't know why they push against me; I implore you, do leave me alone.[66]

As in Lichberg's *Lolita*, the surreal swelling prefigures an outbreak of murderous rage. On both occasions it is jealousy which unleashes the murder, though in the new neighbour's case jealousy that is only simulated; the real motive is hatred of the average lump for the fine-spun outsider. That the brothers have 'fecal matter' instead of grey cells under their skull – rather a crude image by Nabokov's standards – indicates the intensity of his feelings in this story. It is plain that old antipathies mingled here with new impressions from the year 1933. Nabokov himself wrote later that the story originated under the

---

term 'leonardo' for a forger in the 1970s, when he rendered the tale into English with his son: *Stories*, p. 649.

[66] *Stories*, p. 357.

grotesque and ferocious shadow of Hitler.[67] If he had the brothers Walzer in his mind's eye in depicting his swollen German thugs, would their inventor have been a beam in it?

---

[67] Ibid., p. 649. The assertion is untypical for Nabokov, who always resisted the imputation of direct political references in his work, even when they were plain for all to see, as in *Bend Sinister*.

ATOMITE AND THE WIZARD OF OS

That Nabokov could really have meant Lichberg is suggested by another, still more remarkable resemblance. If we leaf through *The Accursed Gioconda* a little further, four stories after *Lolita* we come upon 'Atomit', the penultimate tale in the collection. It contains, to our astonishment, nothing less than the plot of – *The Waltz Invention*.

Heinz von Lichberg's 'Atomit' narrates, in just ten pages, the following story. An inventor by the name of Bobby strolls into the United States War Department and hands over a letter and his card. He is taken to an antechamber and after a long wait, holding two packages, is ushered in to see President Wilkins. Asked by Wilkins what he can do, he replies: 'I can end any war in a day!' Wilkins takes him for mad: 'My good man, you are either a clown or sick!' But Bobby will show him that he is not bluffing. When the President tries to open his boxes, he replies: 'If you go any further, we will both be dead in a second, and the whole Department in perhaps thirty.' For in them is a gram of atomite: 'This gram is fully enough to kill some hundred thousand men in about a minute, if they were standing closely enough together!'

And the plainly not-so-mad Bobby gets ready to prove the power of his hellish machine. The demonstration, to which a mouse in a glass jar falls victim, convinces President Wilkins, who summons a Colonel Rosecamp and his servant Pebbs. A test of the new weapon on larger creatures is agreed for the next day. The inventor is already imagining himself a future multimillionaire. The following morning the test is successful: by remote control a quarter of a gram of atomite is released into the atmosphere, and 'before the faint explosion could even be heard, the animals were lying at the posts to which they were tied, and moved no longer'. But a further trial, in which a still greater quantity is released, ends in disaster. Through the inexperience of the ladies who arrive too late and inadvertently set off the weapon, it is not the animals selected for the experiment but the assembled men who are killed, so that in the future, too, war 'will last somewhat longer than a single day'.

Compressed, such is the dreadfully silly (and dreadfully misogynist) humorous tale 'Atomit', in which – as in Lichberg's 'Lolita' – the first contours of a work by Nabokov appear to be sketched. For how does *The Waltz Invention*, to whose prophetic 'atomystique' Nabokov later proudly pointed, begin?[68]

A man presents himself at the War Ministry and extols a machine he has invented to unleash an explosion of unim-

---

[68] See his foreword to the English-language edition of 1966.

aginable power. Indeed, when this new-fangled weapon is deployed in the third act, an entire city is wiped out – 'Six hundred thousand! In one instant!'[69] Naturally, at the beginning the Minister does not believe a word the inventor says. He takes him for 'just plain crazy' or, indeed, a 'clown!'[70] – until, that is, the inventor offers his first proof by blowing up a mountain at a distance. In this first demonstration too, only small creatures are killed – not a trivial mouse, as in 'Atomit', but elegant lizards (at the end of Lichberg's story, a donkey is mentioned; in Nabokov, it is a 'snow-white gazelle'[71]). After this initial demonstration, interest in acquiring the wonder-weapon grows by leaps and bounds. The Minister – he too accompanied by a Colonel and a servant (not Pebbs, but 'Hump')[72] – realizes the advantages possession of such a remote-controlled weapon would afford. Further tests are agreed with the inventor, which prove equally successful. The last doubts removed, the millions the inventor of 'Atomit' had prematurely hoped for are promptly offered to Walzer/Waltz.

But the latter refuses them, and the paths of the tale and the

---

[69] *The Waltz Invention*, p. 81.

[70] Ibid., pp. 17–18.

[71] As apt a symbol of the difference between the two authors as anyone could find.

[72] 'Hump: an undersized mute – a servant; a general and herald; a sports-instructor' reads his description in the Dramatis Personae of the play. The use of droll names, overworked by Nabokov, is already there in Lichberg. In revising the play, Nabokov dropped the idea of deriving the name of the eleven generals from the 'mountain' [*Berg*].

play separate. Nabokov's continuation shows his hero's rise and fall, his apparent domination of the world, and his final unmasking. For in reality, Waltz/Walzer has sat through all three acts in the Minister's waiting-room (where Bobby had already waited almost two hours), and only dreamt of the action in the play. *In toto* Nabokov develops something that is entirely his own out of Lichberg's scenario – assuming he knew it – and enriches it in an unpredictable way. His world-destroying weapon is no poison gas, but an early atomic bomb.[73] His main character is a poor addled fellow who wraps

---

[73] Lichberg's 'Atomit' was less prophetic; the idea of gas warfare was familiar to every soldier in the First World War. It also plays a brief but dramatic role in a Russian novel that could be another source for *The Waltz Invention*, since it too deals with the invention of a new-fangled weapon capable of annihilating from afar. Its author was Alexei Tolstoy, whose bestseller *The Garin Death Ray* was published in 1927, with an enlarged and revised edition appearing in 1938, thus just prior to the publication of *Izobretenie Val'sa*. Nabokov was personally acquainted with the author, who had frequented his father's house in Berlin and whose openly pro-Soviet attitude he detested. Virtually everything in Tolstoy's novel, in which noble-minded Bolsheviks heroically save the world from the Dostoevskyan genius Garin and a wicked American chemical tycoon, would have disgusted him – which does not mean he never read the book: it is very probable that he did. In Tolstoy, who was technically much more informed than Salvator Waltz, the atom bomb is at least conversationally anticipated. Garin's actual invention is yet more prophetic than Waltz's, a kind of long-distance laser that prefigures Star Wars. The element of plot similarity is the idea that world domination is to be achieved with the help of an ingenious long-distance weapon. But Tolstoy's novel lacks any of the scenic details that *The*

himself in dreams of omnipotence, through whose holes bitter realities eventually whistle. In short, Nabokov's play is a multilayered work of art, and his deluded inventor Salvator Walzer is no caricature, but a character. Yet that is just it: his name remains Waltz/Walzer, and Nabokov even gives him a double, as if he not only did not want to tear the seal of origin from the cousins, but in fact wanted to hang it around their necks for all to see – fifteen years before he wrote a novel on the child-woman who makes her début here as Annabella.[74]

If we put all this together, we find in Nabokov, grouped

Waltz Invention has in common with 'Atomit'. The ending of the novel, on the other hand, which depicts the flight of the dictator Garin from his palace, vaguely resembles Kinbote's flight from Zembla in *Pale Fire*. That one of Garin's *doppelgänger* is a 'Baron Korf' would have amused Nabokov, who devotes some pages of his autobiography to the family of his German great-grandfather, Baron Ferdinand von Korff. (I would like to thank Tatiana Ponomareva, director of the Nabokov museum in St Petersburg, for drawing Alexei Tolstoy's novel to my attention.)

[74] This Annabella, in no way a secondary character, procures the key to the whole play. She is, in effect, subtly equated with Waltz/Walzer's invention. She too is only 'more or less real', as the Dramatis Personae tells us. When the deluded inventor presses her father for her whereabouts, he is told: 'Don't bother to search; she is just as well hidden as your machine.' Girl and invention have the same, twice-mentioned top price. Waltz/Walzer is offered two million for his weapon: 'one million before delivery and one million after'. In the next act, he in turn offers two million for Annabella; 'one right now, the other on delivery'. The girl, in other words, is the real delusion, and the hellish machine, as he confesses in his final outburst, 'is with me, in my pocket, in my breast': *The Waltz Invention*, pp. 63, 108, 111.

around the Lolita-theme, not only the name of Lichberg's brothers, elevated to title status, but also particular grotesque scenes and a sketch for a plot from their immediate vicinity. One has to be quite stubborn a champion of coincidence to dismiss these similarities as mere chance.

All the more so as in *Ada* Nabokov finally lays his cards on the table – or so a proponent of this third hypothesis could argue. For in this novel there really is a work called *Lolita* that is attributed not to Nabokov, but to an author whose name ends in 'berg'. This figure wins a court case because he can prove that passages from his book have been lifted in a film. In this film, which heralds the tragic climax of the novel, Ada plays a Spanish girl by the name of Dolores.

In other words: we have a book, *Lolita*, which someone other than, shall we say, Vivian Darkbloom has written. We have the Spanish (not Mexican or American) child-woman of the same name. We have a court case of plagiarism. And we have as the real *Lolita*-author a gentleman whose name is – no, not Lichberg, but Osberg.[75] Could Nabokov have been more unambiguous?

---

[75] See *Ada*, p. 488. 'For the big picnic on Ada's twelfth birthday . . . the child was permitted to wear her lolita (thus dubbed after the little Andalusian gipsy of that name in Osberg's novel and pronounced, incidentally, with a Spanish "t", not a thick English one . . .)' (p. 77). The film in which Ada plays the young Dolores plagiarizes details from Osberg's short story 'La Gitanella' – according to Boyd the title of *Lolita* in Antiterra (See Boyd, Ada Online: http://www.libraries.psu.edu/nabokov/ada/index.htm). Van's father introduces a side-motif into this thematic complex, consorting with ever younger 'Spanish nymphets' in his old age, until he ends with a ten-year-old.

But – opponents of this hypothesis can immediately point out – Nabokov *was* quite unambiguous, in the notes he attached to the novel. There he helpfully explains to us that the name Osberg is a 'good-natured anagram'. For Osberg read Borges; and to this Borges, with whom he had been compared one time too often, Nabokov pays a somewhat tart tribute. That he really did mean Borges when he wrote Osberg is shown by his characterization of him in the narrative itself as a 'Spanish writer of pretentious fairy-tales and mystico-allegoric anecdotes, highly esteemed by short-shrift thesialists': which captures the Argentinian as Nabokov saw him accurately, if also maliciously, enough.[76] So Osberg is Borges – as has been the undisputed reading since the novel appeared. It has the certificate and seal of the author, and the question remains only whether the matter is thereby settled. The supporters of the third hypothesis would answer no, and raise counter-questions. Just what did Borges have to do with Spanish nymphets? Only in Lichberg is there a Spanish Lolita, and only in him is there a male pair called Walzer, who as 'Walter' recur again in *Ada*.[77] The one allusion, *en plus*, does not exclude the other. *Lolita* was

---

[76] *Ada*, pp. 594, 344.

[77] In Ada's family there are two Walter D. Veens. Brian Boyd, whose commentary on *Ada* produces other, more direct allusions to *The Waltz Invention*, misses this reference back to the play in which 'Walter Walzer' makes his first entrance. In a subtle, if also – as often in *Ada* – barely intelligible balancing act, the original 'Walzer' is turned back into Spanish. Ada explains that her circular marblings would be called 'waltzes' in California '(''because the señorita will dance all night'')': *Ada*, p. 105.

already cryptic enough; *Ada* is a labyrinth. Any philologist who ventured to propose conjectures as remote as those of Vivian Darkbloom in his notes to *Lolita* would be accused of referential mania. Yet Darkbloom is still operating under cover. As Brian Boyd has shown, among the wild luxuriance of allusions in *Ada*, some have as much as a fourfold meaning. One cannot therefore exclude the possibility that the wizard Nabokov had more than one writer in mind when he invented the name 'Osberg' – which would even fit quite well, if we only think of Osram.[78]

One can exclude it even less in that there is no end to name-play after *Ada*. In Nabokov's last novel, *Look at the Harlequins!*, the travesty of an autobiography, Humbert and Lolita appear under other names. The narrator, Vadim, is called Dumbert Dumbert; the eleven-year-old girl on his lap, with whom he meets and falls in love in 1933, is called, like Lolita, 'Dolly'.[79] Dolly's surname is 'von Borg' – the aristocratic prefix *von* retained in the English original. Had it been Nabokov's aim to divide his interpreters once again into camps, he could not have found a more appropriate name. For as naturally as the question arises – is someone juggling with the hot potato of a certain

---

[78] Those who are sceptical about any connection with Lichberg may regard this as a malicious invention; but it is no more and no less than an orchid bloom of coincidence that 'Os' can stand for 'Light'. For Osmium is the name of the chemical element used in the filaments of a light bulb. To complete Lichberg as 'Lichtberg' is an almost automatic slip. The chair of the American Philological Association herself has become a ready victim of it. See Elaine Fantham, 'On Lolita and the Problems of Plagiarism', p. 1.

[79] *Look at the Harlequins!*, Vintage Books, New York, 1974 p. 143.

aristocratic name here? – comes the equally prompt retort from the other side: but no, 'von Borg' is once again Borges, this time not shaken into an anagram, but castrated.

The ambiguity is not to be resolved. Matters would remain there, had not Nabokov brought still other names into play. Dolly von Borg has a pseudo-double called 'Dalberg' – last syllable and stress as in the original.[80] That seems, in total, a bit much: the names of the generals in *The Waltz Invention* that all end in -berg (at a time when Nabokov had never heard of Borges), then Osberg, von Borg, Dalberg, and all linked to Lolita.

Supporters of the third hypothesis have strong evidence on their side. Yet the answer it delivers poses a cluster of new questions, the central one of which is: *why?* For a theme that pounded and gnawed within him for so long, Nabokov certainly had no need of Heinz von Lichberg. As for artistic respect for him, he had – or would have had – equally little. It is one thing to allude to Proust, Poe or Pushkin, to Shakespeare, Flaubert or Joyce, to quote half-sentences or whole plots from them as rich linings to your own work. But what would be the point of embroidering into it an unknown author, and so paying reverence to him? This is the trickiest question in this whole affair, and the right answer may still be beyond us. If we do not believe in the huge, hundred-legged spider of coincidence,

---

[80] Ibid., p. 139. The real name of the girl, with whom Dolly is mixed up, is Talbot, but a baby-sitter gives out the name on the telephone as 'Tallbird or Dalberg'. The mix-up serves only to throw the latter name into the equation.

there is scarcely a way of avoiding the supposition of a some-what more definite acquaintance between Nabokov and the author of *The Accursed Gioconda*. There are many possibilities here – too many even to be delimited.[81] Something may have

---

[81] These possibilities should be pointed out only because the legend is widespread that for fifteen years in Berlin Nabokov had no contact wih Germans. For Véra especially the couple's separation from the outside world in Berlin, not completely hermetic even for Vladimir, was highly porous – she worked, as *The Gift* has immortalized it, in a German office, took speeches by Nazi Ministers down in shorthand, mingled at dances with 'the German elite and numerous members of the diplomatic corps'; rode in the Tiergarten, learnt to shoot, took flying lessons and wanted at one time to become a pilot . . . (see Schiff, *Véra*, pp. 4, 32, 67). If fate had been so minded, it would have had a range of options here to bring her into contact with Herr von Eschwege-Lichberg. The latter could equally have written a piece on the Russian cabaret in Berlin, or a presentation by Sirin at the English–French club; have played at the tennis club in Dahlem of which Nabokov was a member; have frequented one of the aristocrats, Von Dallwitz or Von Bardeleben, of whom the Nabokovs were at one time or another sub-tenants. Véra and Vladimir, whose tale *Time and Ebb* ends with an apotheosis of the early aeroplanes, could have taken an interest in the Zeppelin's journey round the world (which was covered in detail by *Rul'*, the Russian-language daily in Berlin that was Nabokov's main literary out-let). Further possibilities for research are in no way exhausted, though no doubt without the help of coincidence we shall never find out whether the haystack really does contain a needle. That Lichberg knew the name Sirin we may moreover assume; as a journalist he would have read the compe-tition, and it would not have escaped him that the *Vossische Zeitung* serialized two works by Nabokov–Sirin: in July 1928 *Mary*, and in March 1930 *King, Queen, Knave*. Both novels were published in German by Ullstein Verlag.

linked Sirin to Herr von Lichberg, though it would certainly not have been sympathy. Just as in his novels he almost compulsively – and careless even of costs to his narrative – had to introduce gibes at Freud or Dostoevsky and a dozen more of his pet aversions – most of whom, in one way or another, were not so entirely distant from him – so again and again he seems to have reverted to this German who wrote about a nymphet. Yet, we may ask, would he really have condescended so far as to take over Lichberg's names? Or was he so completely confident that he was a snow-white gazelle and the other a donkey that he enjoyed playing with his wretched predecessor and allowing himself risky, triumphant, semi-private jokes at his expense?

This suspicion becomes almost irresistible, if we read the film script of *Lolita* that Nabokov wrote in Hollywood in 1960, into which he smuggled little details that are not to be found in the novel. In one scene Lolita displays her dancing costume to the new tenant and spins charmingly around in front of him, until Humbert admonishes her: 'Hold it, Lolita. No waltzes.' A stage direction lets fall another name: 'In the early light, a smile plays over her flickering lips, like that of a little Gioconda.' Damned little Gioconda! Or this scene: Lolita, sitting with two girls by a swimming-pool, is asked: 'Aren't you kind of Spanish, Lolita? LOLITA (*laughs, shrugging her shoulders*)'. Once again we may ask: who is really laughing at whom here? But, as we can see, with such surmises we gradually leave the terrain of philology for that of psychology, where no certainties can be expected – least of all in the case of a writer who was not just an incalculable genius, but a genius of deception to boot.

We should not deceive ourselves, then, that clarity is to be had where more than enough cloud-banks remain. This is no tall tale, but a story with many unresolved questions – for the time being, and possibly for ever. If the first issue of textual genesis were to be settled by some unequivocal proof, once and for all, the second and third, more sublime and more interesting questions would finally come into their own: what the Ur-Lolita means for the status of Nabokov's novel (not so much), whether it diminishes Nabokov's rank as a writer (but no), whether we need to correct our image of him (slightly), whether we learn something from the two Lolitas about the interplay between high and light literature (absolutely), anything about his relationship to Germans (that too), anything about his art of controlling and sometimes misleading his admirers (certainly). Only one thing is sure: this is the story of an ugly duckling and a proud swan – but if this image smacks too much of a fairy-tale, it can be expressed more technically. Heinz von Lichberg busied himself in his *Lolita*, rather awkwardly, with linen, wood, paper and string. Vladimir Nabokov used similar materials. But out of them he fashioned a kite that would vanish into the clear blue air of literature.

APPENDIX I

TWO STORIES BY HEINZ VON LICHBERG

LOLITA

Someone threw the name of E.T.A. Hoffmann into the conversation. *Musical Tales*.

The young hostess Beate put the orange that she was about to peel back on her plate and said to the young poet: 'Do you think it possible that these stories, which I really read very seldom, keep me awake for nights on end? Common sense tells me that it is all fantasy, and yet . . .'.

'Precisely because it is no fantasy, my dear lady.'

The legation councillor smiled good-humouredly. 'But you don't mean to say that Hoffmann experienced those fearful things?'

'That is exactly what I mean,' rejoined the poet. 'He experienced them! Naturally not with his hands and eyes, but because he was a poet, he experienced what he wrote – or rather, he wrote only of what he experienced in his mind. In fact one could distinguish poets and writers by this criterion. In a poet's mind, this is where fantasy transposes thought into reality!'

It had grown quite silent in the beautiful Countess Beate's little Empire dining-room.

'You are absolutely right,' said the boyish, sensitive-looking professor. 'I would like to tell you about something I have carried around with me for many years now, and I still don't know whether it is experience or fantasy. But it will take a moment or two.'

'Please go ahead,' said his hostess.

And so the scholar began his story:

'Towards the end of the last century I was a student in a very old, fairly large town in South Germany. This must have been some twenty years ago. I lived, since it appealed to me, in a narrow street lined with very old houses. Near my lodgings there was a small tavern that must be one of the strangest I have ever seen. I often went there in the late autumn afternoons, when I would take a break from my work before the last of the daylight had gone.

'It consisted of just a single dilapidated room with a low ceiling gathering shadows. By the windows on to the street stood two immaculately scrubbed tables with hard wooden chairs. At the back, in a dark corner by the tiled stove, stood a third little table flanked by two strange armchairs covered in brightly coloured chintz. A black silk headscarf of the sort Spanish girls wear on days of celebration was draped over the armchair next to the stove. I never saw another patron in there besides myself, and even today I cannot rid myself of the idea that it wasn't a public tavern at all. The front door, in any event, was locked, and the shutters on the windows closed every evening on the stroke of seven. I never asked about this, as I soon began to take an unaccountably keen interest in the owners of this curious establishment.

They were called Aloys and Anton Walzer, and appeared very old. Both were incredibly tall and thin, without a hair on their heads but with long, tousled, full grey beards that were streaked with red. I never saw them dressed in anything except yellowish trousers and long baggy black jackets. They were so alike that they must have been twins, and it was only the fact of Anton's having a slightly deeper voice that finally allowed me to tell them apart. When I arrived they would, without asking or saying anything, always bring a glass of wonderful, sweet Spanish wine and set it down for me on the table by the stove with a friendly smile. Aloys unfailingly sat in the armchair next to me, while, as a rule, Anton would stand, leaning his back against the window. Both smoked a highly aromatic tobacco in the sort of pipes you often see in Flemish engravings. They always seemed to be waiting for something.

'If I said that the two old men made a grotesque impression on me, that would be misleading, since the word grotesque implies a certain absurdity. No, the impression that the Walzers produced was of something unspeakably weary, fearful, and all but tragic.

'There did not appear to be a female presence living in the house – at least, I never noticed any sign of one.

'A visit to the smoke-filled parlour soon became an essential part of every day's routine, especially when winter set in, with its early dusks and long evenings. I became increasingly familiar to the owners, and from time to time they would engage me in brief conversation. But they seemed to have lost all sense of the present, only ever speaking of times long gone in voices that sounded curiously parched and grating. I told them about my travels, and each time the conversation turned to southern lands, a wary, unsettled glint stole into their eyes, occasionally overlaid with a hint of wistful expectation. Then they would seem to be living in a memory. I could never leave the tavern without the vague feeling that something awful was about to happen after I'd gone – and naturally, time and again I'd then smile at such notion.

'One evening I passed their establishment quite late and heard, behind the shuttered windows, a violin softly playing an exquisite melody that so captivated me that I remained standing outside in the street for a long time. The next day, when I asked the old men what it was, they just smiled and shook their heads.

'Several weeks went by and then, one night, I passed their windows again – perhaps at an even later hour this time. I heard such wild shouting coming from behind the shutters, such indescribable cursing and swearing, that I froze, appalled. The voices were definitely coming from the tavern, there was no doubt about that, but it couldn't have been the two old men locked in violent argument, because, however furious, their voices could never have sounded so deep or youthful or loud. Two young, strong people must have been at each other's throats in there.

'The shouts grew ever louder, rising to a pitch of uncontrollable exasperation as every now and then a fist slammed down on to a table with a crash.

'All of sudden a silvery, feminine laugh rang out, and then the infuriated voices swelled to an insane roar.

'I stood there rooted to the spot, not even thinking for a moment to open the door and look to see what was happening.

'Then the woman's voice gave a scream – a little scream, but one of such fright, of such awful dread, that I still have not forgotten it today. Then everything became quiet.

'When I walked in the next day, Anton brought a glass of wine to my table with his customary friendly smile, and everything was so unchanged that I began to think it had all been a dream, and I was ashamed to ask the old men.

'It was towards the end of winter that I was obliged to explain to the brothers one afternoon that I wouldn't be able to come any more, because I was setting off for Spain the following day.

'My announcement appeared to have a strange effect on Anton and Aloys, for their hard, picturesquely ugly faces turned pale, and they looked down at the ground. They left the room and I heard them whispering to one another outside. After a while Anton came back in and asked me agitatedly whether I would be going to Alicante as well, and when I replied that I would, he scurried out to his brother with comical haste. After a further while, they came back in and acted as if nothing had happened.

'I forgot about the old men as I finished my preparations for the trip, but that night I had a vague, confused dream in which a small, crooked, salmon-coloured house in one of the disreputable streets leading down to Alicante's harbour played a part.

'When I went to the station the next day, I noticed that Anton and Aloys' shutters were firmly shut in broad daylight.

'But once I was under way, immersed in my work, I soon forgot about these insignificant events in South Germany. One forgets so easily when one travels.

'I stayed in Paris for a few days to visit some friends and poke around the Louvre. One evening, tired from looking, I went to a cabaret in the Quartier Latin to hear one of those curious *chansonniers* who an acquaintance of mine had promised me was a true artist. I found a very old, blind man with a grave, mournful voice, who, it was true, sang quite beautifully and was expertly accompanied by his pretty daughter on the violin.

'After a while she took to the stage alone, and suddenly I recognized the exquisite melody that had amazed me weeks before when I had heard it coming from the Walzers' tavern in the middle of the night. I asked what it was, and was told that it was a gavotte by Giovanni Lully from the reign of Louis XIV.

'A few days later I set off for Lisbon, and at the beginning of February I travelled to Alicante by way of Madrid.

'I have always had a weakness for the South – and for Spain above all. One is raised to a higher power there, if I may so put it: everything is experienced in its most intense form, and all of life becomes sultry and unrestrained under the glare of the sun. The people are like their wine, which is strong, fiery and sweet, but quick to effervesce and dangerously choleric when it ferments. Then, too, I have always had the feeling that every southerner has a little of Don Quixote's blood in his veins.

'I had nothing special to do in Alicante, in fact. But I love those ineffably sweet nights on the harbour when the moon hangs over the Castle of Santa Barbara and throws everything into stark, ghostly contrast. In every German there lies a streak of lyrical sentimentality just waiting for such occasions. The moment I entered the town on muleback, the memory of the Walzer brothers and their curious establishment returned to me with absurd vividness. Of course this may be fancy, or rewriting after the event, but I seemed to steer my mule almost involuntarily past the Algorfa palace and down to the harbour. There, in one of the old streets where the sailors live, I found the lodgings I was looking for.

'Severo Ancosta's *pension* was a small, crooked building with large balconies squeezed in between identical neighbours. The friendly, talkative landlord gave me a room with a wonderful view of the sea, and nothing stood in the way of my enjoying a week of undisturbed beauty.

'Until, on the second day, I saw *Lolita*, Severo's daughter.

'By our northern standards she was terribly young, with veiled southern eyes and hair of an unusual reddish gold. Her body was boyishly slim and supple, and her voice full and dark. But there was something more than her beauty that attracted me – there was a strange mystery about her that often troubled me on those moonlit nights.

'When she tidied up in my room, she would sometimes stop

in the middle of her work, press her red, laughing lips into two narrow lines, and stare fearfully at the sun. Then she had the air of an Iphigenia played by a great tragedienne. At such moments I always felt an overpowering need to take the child in my arms and shield her from some unknown danger.

'There were days when Lolita's big shy eyes regarded me with an unspoken question, and there were evenings when I saw her burst into sudden uncontrollable sobs.

'I had ceased to think of travelling on. I was entranced by the South – and Lolita. Golden hot days and silvery melancholy nights.

'And then came the evening of unforgettable reality and dreamlike magic as Lolita sat on my balcony and sang softly, as she often did. But this time she came to me with halting steps on the landing, the guitar discarded precipitously on the floor. And while her eyes sought out the image of the flickering moon in the water, like a pleading child she flung her trembling little arms around my neck, leant her head on my chest, and began sobbing. There were tears in her eyes, but her sweet mouth was laughing. The miracle had happened. ''You are so strong,'' she whispered.

'Days and nights came and went; the mystery of beauty held them entwined in an unchanging, singing serenity.

'Then the days became weeks, and I began to realize that I must travel on. Not because any duty called me, but because Lolita's outsized, dangerous love filled me with fear. When I told her, she regarded me with an indescribable expression and nodded mutely. Then suddenly she seized my hand and bit it with all the strength of her little mouth. These scars of love have remained indelible even twenty-five years later.

'Before I could say anything, Lolita had disappeared into the house. I saw her only once more. . . .

'That evening, on the bench by the front door, I had a serious conversation with Severo about his daughter.

' "Come, sir," he said. "I want to show you something and tell you the whole story." He led me upstairs to a room, which was separated from mine only by a door. I stopped in amazement.

'The boxy, low room had no other furniture than a small table and three armchairs. But these chairs were the same, or almost the same, as the armchairs in the Walzer brothers' tavern. And at that moment I knew that it was Severo Ancosta's house that I had seen in my dreams the night before I left Germany!

'On the wall hung a drawing of Lolita that was so true to life that I went over to examine it up close.

' "You think that's Lolita," smiled Severo, "but it's Lola, the grandmother of Lolita's great-grandmother, who was strangled by her lovers after a quarrel a hundred years ago!"

'We sat down and in his friendly way, Severo told me the story. He spoke of Lola, who was the most beautiful woman of her day in the town – so beautiful that the men who loved her were doomed to die. Shortly after the birth of her daughter she was murdered by two of her lovers, whom she had tormented to the point of insanity.

'Ever since then the family had been under a sort of curse. The women only ever had one daughter, and always went insane a number of weeks after the birth of their child. But they were all beautiful – as beautiful as Lolita!

' "That is how my wife died," he said in a grave whisper, "and that is how my daughter will die!"

'I could hardly find words to comfort him, for anxiety for my little Lolita flooded over me.

'When I went to my room that evening, I found a small flower I didn't recognize on the pillow on my bed. Lolita's farewell gift, I thought to myself, and took it in my hand. Then I saw that it was really white, and red only with Lolita's blood.

'That was the way she loved.

'I couldn't sleep that night. A thousand dreams pursued me, and suddenly – it was probably around midnight – a terrible thing happened. The door of the adjoining room flew open, and I saw three people sitting in the chairs around the table in the middle of the room. Two young, strong, blond lads on either side, and Lolita in the middle. But it was Lola, not Lolita – or was it Lolita, after all?

'Glasses of dark-red wine stood before them on the table. The girl was laughing loudly and playfully, but there was a hard, scornful line about her mouth. Then the two men took up their violins and played. And I felt the blood pulse faster in my veins as the violins sang out the familiar melody, the old gavotte from the time of the Sun King.

'When it was over, the woman wantonly dashed her glass to the floor and gave another cooing, silvery laugh. Then one of the lads, who was sitting facing me, set his violin on the table and shouted: "And now tell us which one of us you will choose!"

'She laughed. "The most handsome. But you are both so handsome. You have a foreign, cold beauty that we don't know here."

'The other shouted even louder. "Do you want him or do you want me? Tell us, woman, or by God . . .!"

' "Do you love me?" she asked expectantly. "You all love me! But if your love is really so great, then you will fight for me with all the strength of your desire, and I will ask the Virgin to send a miracle to show me whose love is the strongest. Will you do that?"

' "Yes," said the lads, and hostilely looked each other in the eye.

' "*I will love the one who is strongest!*"

'So they took off their jackets and their muscles swelled. But they realized that they were equally strong.

' "*I will love the one who is tallest!*" Her eyes flashed.

'And lo and behold, the men grew taller and taller, their necks lengthened and grew thinner and their sleeves burst right through to their elbows. Their faces became ugly and distorted, and I thought I could hear their bones cracking. But not by so much as a hair did one become larger than the other. Then they banged their deformed fists on the table, knocking the violins on to the floor, and set to blaspheming.

' "*I will love the older of you!*" she shrieked.

'Their hair fell out, deep furrows lined their faces, their hands became weak and tremulous and their knees shook as they struggled painfully to their feet, drooling, in a frenzy of agitation. The venom in their eyes was dulled, and their stentorian bellows of rage and disappointment came out as hoarse cries. "By God, you shrew," croaked one of them. "Decide! Decide – or you go to hell with your thrice-cursed beauty!"

'Then she slumped forward laughing over the table and cried out, with tears in her eyes:, *"I will love the one – I will love the one who has the longest, ugliest beard!"*

'Long red hairs sprouted from the men's distorted faces as they let out bestial, crazed shrieks of fury and despair. Raising their fists, they bore down on the woman, as she tried to get away. But in an instant the two of them had fallen upon her and were strangling her with their long, bony fingers.

'I couldn't move. A numbing cold spread up my spine, and I had to shut my eyes. When I opened them again, I saw that the two men in the next room, who were standing over the victim of their revenge with mad looks in their eyes, were Anton and Aloys Walzer.

'Then I lost all consciousness.

'I did not come to again until the sun was shining brightly into my room, and I saw that the door to the adjoining room was shut. I pulled it open and found everything as it had been the evening before. Except that I thought I remembered a thin layer of dust on the furniture, which was no longer there, and there seemed to be a faint smell of wine in the air.

'An hour later I walked out on to the street and saw Severo coming towards me, pale and distraught. Tears stood in his eyes.

' "Lolita died last night," he said softly.

'I cannot describe what happened to me at these words, and if I could it would be a profanity for me to speak of it.

'My beloved little Lolita lay in her small, narrow bed with her eyes wide open. Her teeth were clenched convulsively in her lower lip, and her fragrant blonde hair lay tangled.

'I don't know what she died of. In my boundless confusion I forgot to ask. But it was certainly not from the small cut on her golden-brown left arm. That had only stained the white flower red, for my sake.

'I closed her tender little eyes and then knelt and buried my head in her cool hand; I don't know for how long. The next thing I knew, Severo had come in and reminded me that my steamer to Marseilles was leaving in an hour.

'I left.

'When the ship was already far out to sea, I recognized the outlines of Santa Barbara once more. Then it struck me that this sharp-angled castle would now see them lay her beloved little body in the ground. I could not prevent my eyes and my heart beseech the tall towers with a force of yearning I had never known before: "Remember me to her, remember me to her at the last – and always! Always!"

'But Lolita's soul I took with me.

'It was only years later that I returned to the old South German town. A horrible woman who dealt in seed now lived in the Walzers' little tavern. I asked her about the brothers and learnt that on the morning after the night Lolita died, they were both found dead in the armchairs by the stove with a friendly smile on their faces.'

The scholar, whose gaze had darted questioningly about the plates as he spoke, looked up.

After a while, the Countess Beate opened her eyes. 'You are a poet,' she said, and swiftly held out her hand to him, so that the bracelets jingled on her thin wrist.

ATOMITE

'Well, well,' said Bobby Kennyson, rapping on the steel box. 'What a stroke of luck the old man made me do chemistry all those years ago! I'd like to see if any other fellow can copy this. I'm going to be mighty rich if – well, we'll find out about that right now!'

Then he clapped his pal Bill Stakes on the shoulder with his big paw, which was his way of saying 'Goodbye', jammed his hat on his head, and rushed out with his packages.

He went straight to the War Department of the United States of America, where he presented a letter and his card.

The servant looked them over, and then said slyly, 'Invention, eh?'

'Naturally,' boomed Bobby. 'What else?'

'Then you'll probably have to wait a bit – you're number 29 today.' Bobby was shown into a room where a dozen or so men sat on chairs, all with packages on their knees. They broke off their animated conversations and looked intently as one at

Bobby, who sat down rather taken aback. Then the talk resumed.

After an hour and forty minutes, the servant came in and whispered to him: 'You're to come through to Mr Graham Wilkins,' and led the way. Bobby was ushered into a room where the man responsible for inspecting inventions sat behind a desk. He wore glasses and had a strong, clean-shaven jaw.

Little did Bobby suspect that this surly hero moonlighted as President of the Society for the Reduction of American Inventions. But even so, Mr Graham Wilkins' baleful stare made Bobby entirely forget the beautiful speech he had planned. So instead he put his box on the table, set a second package on the floor, and twisted his shabby hat in his hands.

'What can you do?' the stern official commanded him.

'I can . . .,' stuttered Bobby, 'I can end any war in a day!'

'My good man, you are either a clown or sick!' roared Mr Wilkins, and reached out to open the box.

'If you go any further, we will both be dead in a second, and the whole Department in perhaps thirty,' Bobby remarked matter-of-factly.

Mr Wilkins snatched back his hands as if he'd been bitten and sat down again, shaken.

'For in this box,' Bobby continued, emboldened, 'there is a gram of atomite. This gram is fully enough to kill some hundred thousand men in about a minute, if they were standing closely enough together!'

'But how can a hundred thousand men eat a gram?' the square-jawed inspector asked suspiciously.

'Atomite is not eaten,' Bobby replied proudly. 'It is inhaled. A minuscule particle of atomite will destroy a man's windpipe and lungs in a trice. I will now demonstrate this to you.

'You see this jar. At the bottom, there's an ordinary mouse. At the top, in this lid, there is a tiny piece of cotton wool, which I have exposed to the atomite. By pressing this lever, I will release the cotton wool and you may observe the effects.'

He stuck three thick plasters over the air holes through which the little mouse had been breathing up till then, and fitted a metal lid on top.

'But the mouse is sweating, and already half dead,' Mr Wilkins objected, his interest aroused.

'If you sat in a jar for three hours, wouldn't you break a sweat too?' Bobby pointed out amicably. 'No, please don't worry, stay there. Nothing can happen to you.'

Then he pressed the lever, and a little scrap of cotton wool fluttered down from the lid of the jar right on to the mouse's back. The little animal snapped open its mouth, stretched out its four legs, and was dead.

'Excellent! Unbelievable!' said Mr Wilkins. 'And is the effect on larger creatures the same?'

'As I've already told you, Mr Wilkins.'

'Well, it would be worth a trial,' said the mandarin, and rang a bell. 'Fetch Colonel Rosecamp,' he ordered when the servant entered.

The colonel appeared, and listened to a description of Bobby's invention with amazement. 'I must see this,' he said.

'With pleasure,' said Bobby. 'The equipment for larger-scale trials is all ready. It is now just a question of getting our hands on some large animals.'

'Perhaps we could go in the building opposite,' the Colonel said dryly. 'They're holding a women's election meeting in there now.'

'I've got an idea,' Mr Wilkins touched a finger to his nose, which he always did when he was thinking. 'There's an ancient donkey downstairs in the stable that was put out to pasture ages ago. That would do!'

'Good,' said Rosecamp. 'And we'll get the rest of the animals from the clinics.'

Wilkins rang for the servant. 'Pebbs,' he said, 'we've an old donkey on the premises. Go downstairs, he should . . .'

'I beg your pardon, Mr Wilkins,' Pebbs interrupted, 'but as far as I know Mr Kensing has already gone to lunch!'

The Colonel laughed so hard he had to sit down, and a grin even stole over Mr Wilkins' earnest countenance. 'I did not mean Mr Kensing this time, Pebbs, I want the real donkey with four legs that's down in the stable!'

'Mr Kensing is my private secretary,' he explained, turning to Bobby Kennyson.

Pebbs left to send for the poor old donkey.

The trials were set for the following morning, and Bobby went happily home. On the way, in anticipation of his becoming a multimillionaire, he bought himself a new hat.

At the crack of dawn the following day, a strange caravan wound its way across a field. An old blind horse, the wretched donkey from the War Department and a few dogs, cats and rabbits jolted about in one lorry. In another Mr Wilkins followed with Mr Kensing, Colonel Rosecamp, Bobby, and the latter's assistants. The atomite equipment was stowed in two large crates.

Mrs Mabel Wilkins and Miss Maggie Wilkins had wanted to attend the spectacle too, but naturally hadn't been dressed in time.

When the lorries' passengers had disembarked, Bobby supervised preparations. He took two jars. 'There's a quarter of a gram of atomite in this receptacle and half a gram in this one. There's a small cartridge attached to the lid of each, which I will later detonate by an electrical lead. We'll stand these jars here and tie the test animals to the posts in a circle with a radius of fifty paces. Let's say for the first trial, with a quarter of a gram, we'll take the horse, five cats and three rabbits. There. And now we connect the wire to the cartridge and move away with the other animals to a distance from which we can still observe proceedings clearly.'

So they withdrew and left the animals to their scientific fate.

After five hundred paces – the wires wouldn't reach any further – the gentlemen halted, and Bobby connected the wires to the detonator. 'If I push this button on the left,' he explained, 'I will blow up the jar with the quarter of a gram of atomite, whereas if I push the right one, then the jar with the stronger dose will explode. For the second trial we will put the animals in a circle with a radius of a hundred paces, although atomite, which spreads through the atmosphere with prodigious ease, has a far greater range. But you need not worry, gentlemen, for now I am pouring the contents of this bottle around our position here; it is the only antidote that destroys every trace of atomite instantaneously. The crews of the atomite canons in future wars will use protective masks containing this antidote. And now, gentlemen, could I have your attention!'

He pushed the left button, and before the faint explosion could even be heard, the animals were lying by the posts to which they had been tied, and moved no longer.

'Splendid,' said Mr. Wilkins. 'We'll be able to do away with the electric chair!'

They all made their way to the victims of science to study the effects. Just as they reached the circle where the old donkey and his companions in misfortune stood resigned to their fate near the detonator, two enchanting figures in little white shoes, bright little summer dresses and colourful parasols appeared.

'Oh Maggie,' said Mrs Mabel Wilkins. 'Look, there they are and here is one of their gadgets. It seems to have been worth coming out here after all, despite them being so inconsiderate and not waiting for us. Look what a funny thing this is!'

Maggie hesitantly inspected the detonator with the timidity women have when faced with things they don't understand. 'It's a strange box with two buttons and wires coming out of them!' she said.

The men had caught sight of the women now.

'Look, Maggie, they're waving like crazy and they keep

pointing at you. Your father keeps on shouting,' Mrs Mabel said, in a state of high excitement. 'I think they want you to do something with that thing there.'

At the other end of the field, they had recognized the danger and were signalling wildly.

'Hurry up, Maggie, they're getting more and more angry!'

'Here's a button to push,' Maggie said helplessly.

'Well, push it, then,' ordered her mother. 'You can see how they're shouting for it.'

At that moment the men were frenziedly running in all directions in a bid to save themselves, since they saw what was going to happen.

Maggie pushed.

'Oh, now they're all running in all directions like madmen,' laughed Mrs Mabel. 'Look – oops-a-daisy, now they've all thrown themselves on the ground! Really, these men can't take anything seriously. They always have to play their silly jokes on us! Come on, Maggie, let's go to those silly-billies!'

And so, cutely turned out in their bright little dresses as if they were the first breath of spring itself, the two women tripped over to the men, who lay face down and were no longer moving.

Meanwhile the old donkey, pleased at the turn of events, was trotting back to his stable in town. On the way he said to the dachshund limping along beside him: 'You see, my friend, if it hadn't been for those beautiful women, we'd be dead now! But then humans wouldn't have fought over any bone of contention. As it is, because of those beautiful women, war in the future will last somewhat longer than a single day!'

He was only an old donkey but, given that, he actually spoke very sensibly.

APPENDIX II

WHO WROTE *LOLITA* FIRST?
AN INTERVIEW WITH MICHAEL MAAR

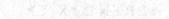

*I*n this conversation – *first published in March 2016 in the German magazine* Cicero – *Daniel Kehlmann and Michael Maar discuss Maar's discoveries about* Lolita.

DANIEL KEHLMANN: *In your book* The Two Lolitas, *you made an intriguing discovery – it started to obsess me a bit. What's equally interesting, and kind of outrageous, is that most Nabokov scholars ignored your finding. Maybe they felt they ought to shield Nabokov from charges of plagiarism. So let's get this out of the way first – is this about plagiarism?*

MICHAEL MAAR: Of course not. The word came up in the press when I published my first article about the discovery, but that's not what this is about at all.

Let me sum it up. Heinz von Lichberg, a writer who's completely forgotten today, and rightly so, published a volume of bad short stories in 1916, The Cursed Gioconda. *In it there's a story called 'Atomit' in which a man develops a doomsday machine that can destroy the world. Nabokov wrote a play in 1938,* The Waltz Invention *— it's about a man who develops a doomsday machine with the potential to destroy the world.*

There's more.

Lichberg's 'Atomit' begins with a scene in which the inventor meets with the US Secretary of Defense to pitch his project. Nabokov's The Waltz Invention *opens in the office of the Minister of Defense of a powerful, unnamed state, where the inventor proceeds to pitch his doomsday machine. Coincidence?*

Possibly. But there's still more.

Nabokov's inventor goes by the name of Waltz. He has a cousin whose name is Waltz, too. In another story from Lichberg's collection, we also find two men who are close relatives — in this case, brothers — and their family name is Walzer, the German word for waltz. The narrator of this story falls in love with a young girl, the daughter of his landlord. A narrator who falls in love with his landlady's daughter — that's something we know very well from Nabokov's Lolita. *And what's the girl's name in Lichberg's story? Lolita. And what's the name of the story? It's 'Lolita.' Written by Heinz von Lichberg and published in 1916.*

The name alone wouldn't prove anything, but if you look at all those other parallels — doomsday machine, inventors, ministers of defense, two relatives called Waltz — it's safe to assume that Nabokov knew Lichberg's book.

It seems to me a rational assumption, but Nabokov scholars are in near-complete denial. One of the few scholars who bothered to react was Dieter E. Zimmer, the editor of Nabokov's Collected Works *in German. He claimed that it's all pure coincidence – but he only mentions a young girl named Lolita. He doesn't mention the Waltz parallels. And Nabokov's biographer Brian Boyd, what did he have to say? Well, not a lot. Quite a while after you made your discovery, he published a book of essays about new developments in Nabokov studies, which neglects to mention Lichberg at all. And recently he explained, in a Nabokov forum online, that there's nothing unusual about two girls coincidentally having the name Lolita in the works of two different writers. Again, no mention of the doomsday machine, the Minister of Defense, the Waltz name. With all due respect, as a great admirer of Nabokov, I feel cheated.*

We have to assume that these scholars are strictly neutral, with no personal interest at stake. But through some of the more heated reactions it became clear that there was one fact about Lichberg that people found hard to stomach – he was an ardent Nazi. He enthusiastically praised Hitler on German radio, his voice trembling with emotion. This was when Hitler became chancellor – you can listen to him on YouTube, if you really want to. Later Lichberg wrote articles for the Nazi paper *Völkischer Beobachter*. It may be hard to accept that Nabokov, who fled from the Nazis with his Jewish wife and whose brother Sergey died in the Neuengamme concentration camp, was linked to that kind of a man.

Nabokov incessantly teases his readers to decode his references — which is why it's clear to me that this isn't about plagiarism. It's about a clear reference, about what Nabokov is trying to signal to us by alluding to the work of an unimportant German writer — a writer we have every reason to assume he would have loathed for literary and personal reasons — at the centre of several of his works. And if this isn't a signal for his readers, who does he want to signal to? That's the question I find hard to ignore, and I find it exasperating that Nabokov scholars keep ignoring it.

There has to be a missing link. It's not improbable, for example, that they knew each other in person. They lived in the same Berlin neighbourhood for about fifteen years. Could Lichberg have been Nabokov's landlord? Could they have been in the same tennis club? They were both good tennis players. I tried to look into that, but the membership lists of the Dahlem tennis clubs were destroyed in the war. Even if they *had* been in the same club, that wouldn't answer your question — what was he trying to signal, and to whom? It doesn't stop with the book, either. In his *Lolita* screenplay, which Kubrick didn't use, he has someone ask whether the girl is Spanish. And when Humbert Humbert exclaims, in the same screenplay, that Lolita is not supposed to be 'dancing a Waltz', or when he gives her 'the smile of a Gioconda'.

Lichberg's story is set in Spain, and the title of his book is The Cursed Gioconda.

Exactly. It does seem like a wink.

But to whom? Lichberg died in 1951 and, anyway, it's very hard to imagine the two of them as friends. Also, some Nabokov scholars have been quite steadfast in their claim that the great man didn't speak German, and if that's true, he couldn't have read Lichberg. But you just need to ask around a bit and you find out that's not true.

Who did you ask?

Gerhard Bronner, a famous Austrian comedian and nightclub owner who died in 2007, told me how, years ago, the Austrian writer Friedrich Torberg brought Nabokov and his cousin Nicolai to Gerhard's bar in the centre of Vienna. Gerhard remembered Vladimir speaking very decent German, albeit with a heavy accent. But I really don't think we even need this kind of anecdotal evidence. In my opinion, the parallels between Nabokov's and Lichberg's works would be enough in themselves to conclude that he must have known those stories – and that it's likely he had some knowledge of German.

And let's not forget that by his own admission he read Thomas Mann and Freud in the original – hating them fiercely, of course. And he did translate Heinrich Heine and Goethe into Russian. If you can do that, reading Lichberg shouldn't be too hard.

The thing I just can't get over here is that Nabokov keeps asking his readers to decode his references. But the Lichberg reference is something he couldn't have assumed would ever get discovered, let alone decoded.

It's certainly puzzling. He liked private jokes, though.

But of course he's famously unforgiving when it comes to his judgment of literary or moral quality — and Lichberg was a bad writer and a Nazi! So why in the world would Nabokov reference him like this? What could have been his intention?

Anybody who offers me a good theory can have my first edition of *The Cursed Gioconda*. Which is a rare book! My personal guess would be that a good private eye could find out. Sorry, I'm just a modest literary critic.

POSTSCRIPT BY MICHAEL MAAR

Only a few weeks after this talk — and one day before the *Paris Review* published it — I was reading Nabokov's *Letters to Véra* and discovered what seems to be the missing link, if not the smoking gun. The copiously annotated letters show that Nabokov and Véra were lodgers at a certain Frau von Bardeleben, in Luitpoldstraße, where they remained from 1929 to 1932 — a relatively long period of time, given Nabokov's lodging habits. Vladimir used to call his landlady 'Mrs Walrus'. She was married to Albrecht von Bardeleben. The Nabokovs seemed to be quite familiar with the von Bardelebens. Even years later, in April 1937, Vladimir responds in a letter to Véra about some funny chat she must have reported: 'How amusing — about Bardelebeness.' Evidently they stayed in touch with their ex-landlords somehow. Otherwise, why would they exchange news about these people five years after they'd moved out? And more interesting still: they knew each other long before he became her lodger. Already in June 1926, Vladimir writes to Véra that he met the Walrus – the nickname indicating a longer acquaintance – and tried to touch her 'little saintly Nuki' (he even knows her dog's name and status). In 1930, Vladimir has a literary conversation with Mrs Walrus, planning to give her his 'King, Queen, Knave', published at Ullstein's, since 'her daughter likes reading Ullstein books'. Little wonder, if the Walrus felt she should return the gift?

There's one genealogical detail the rich annotations in *Letters to Véra* do not reveal. Remember that Heinz von Lichberg, who wrote the first *Lolita*, was the pen name of Heinz von Eschwege. Well, it turns out the Nabokovs' landlords, the von Bardelebens, are related to the von Eschweges – Charlotte von Bardeleben, born in 1766, was married in 1787 to Johann Friedrich Ludwig von Eschwege. In other words: for at least three years Nabokov lived under one roof with the family of his infamous predecessor.

It doesn't take much to imagine the rest. The von Bardelebens and the von Eschweges both belonged to the Hessian high nobility, and nobility weaves a meticulous web: everyone seems to know one another and occasionally to meet. Heinz von Eschwege might have been a regular or sporadic guest at the von Bardelebens; Mrs Walrus might have alerted Nabokov to von Eschwege's books. Or maybe it was the other way around, and Nabokov became a lodger at the von Bardelebens because he was already an acquaintance of Heinz von Eschwege. Research, as they say, is ongoing.

SELECT BIBLIOGRAPHY

von Becker, Peter, 'Nymph-Knoten', *Der Tagesspiegel*, 21 March 2004, p. 26.

Beutler, Philine, 'Kenner und Auskenner. Eine Diebsgeschichte um Peter Hacks, Vladimir Nabokov und Marcel Reich-Ranicki', *Junge Welt*, 7 April 2004.

Breitenstein, Andreas, 'Das doppelte Lottchen', *Neue Zürcher Zeitung*, 22 March 2004, p. 18.

Caldwell, Christopher, 'Who Invented Lolita?', *The New York Times Magazine*, 23 May 2004.

Corino, Karl, 'Die doppelte Lolita', *Rheinischer Merkur*, no. 16, 15 April 2004, p. 17.

Dispot, Laurent, '*Lolita*, Une, Première', *La Règle du Jeu*, pp. 47–51.

Fantham, Elaine, 'On Lolita and the Problems of Plagiarism', *American Philological Association Newsletter*, vol. 27, no. 3, 4 June 2004, pp. 1f.

Handelzalts, Michael, 'Lo. Lee. Ta. Did She Have a Precursor?', *Haaretz*, 6 August 2004.

Hartwig, Ina, ' "Lo.Li.Ta.", süßes Wesen', *Frankfurter Rund-schau*, 14 April 2004, p. 19.

Krause, Tilman, 'Haben Nabokov und Thomas Mann geklaut?', *Die Welt*, 4 May 2004, p. 27.

von Lichberg, Heinz, 'Lolita'. Reprinted in *Frankfurter Allge-meine*, 27 March 2004, p. 39.

von Lichberg, Heinz, 'Lolita', French trans. by Laurent Dispot, *La Régle du Jeu*, no. 25, May 2004, pp. 36–47.

von Lichberg, Heinz, 'Lolita', trans. Carolyn Kunin, *The Times Literary Supplement*, no. 5286, 23 July 2004, pp. 14f.

Maar, Michael, 'Was wußte Nabokov?', *Frankfurter Allgemeine*, 19 March 2004, p. 37.

Maar, Michael, 'Der Mann, der "Lolita" erfand', *Frankfurter Allgemeine*, 26 March 2004, p. 46.

Maar, Michael, 'Curse of the First Lolita', *The Times Literary Supplement*, no. 5270, 2 April 2004, pp. 13–15.

Maar, Michael, 'Lolitas spanische Freundin', *Frankfurter Allge-meine*, 29 April 2004, p. 33.

Maar, Michael, 'A Ninfeta Feia', *mais!*, no. 64, 4 July 2004, pp. 9–12.

Park, Ed, 'Lo-Lee-Huh?', *Village Voice*, 12 April 2004.

Reich-Ranicki, Marcel, 'Eine richtige Entdeckung', *Der Spiegel*, no. 13, 22 March 2004, p. 182.

Rosenbaum, Ron, 'New Lolita Scandal! Did Nabokov Suffer From Cryptomnesia?', *The New York Observer*, 19 April 2004, pp. 1–7.

Schmid, Ulrich M., 'Nabokov lächelt', *Neue Zürcher Zeitung*, 21 April 2004, p. 35.

Steinfeld, Thomas, 'Watson, übernehmen Sie!', *Süddeutsche Zeitung*, 1 April 2004, p. 16.

Walsh, Nick Paton, 'Novel Twist: Nabokov Family Rejects Lolita Plagiarism Claim', *Guardian*, 2 April 2004.

Wittstock, Uwe, 'Lolita ist eigentlich viel älter', *Die Welt*, 20 March 2004, p. 28.

Zimmer, Dieter E., 'Die doppelte Lolita', *Die Zeit*, no. 18, 22 April 2004, p. 57.